Activity Gurus

A Journey To Facilitating Meaningful Activities In Social Care

CLARE COPLESTON & RIGERTA AHMETAJ

Disclaimer

This book is designed to provide information and motivation to our readers. It is sold with the understanding that the author and publisher are not engaged to render any type of psychological, legal, or any other kind of professional advice. The content is the sole expression and opinion of its author. Neither the publisher nor the individual author(s) shall be liable for any physical, psychological, emotional, financial, or commercial damages, including, but not limited to, special, incidental, consequential or other damages. Our views and rights are the same: You are responsible for your own choices, actions, and results.

The content of the book is solely written by the author.

DVG STAR Publishing are not liable for the content of the book.

Published by DVG STAR PUBLISHING

www.dvgstar.com

email us at info@dvgstar.com

ISBN: 1-912547-36-8
ISBN-13: 978-1-912547-36-4

DEDICATION

To my dear friend and prior deputy manager

Mrs Jennifer Taylor

and

In fond memory of 'the Boss'

Mrs Rosemary Sharp

Rest in peace Rose, you may be gone, but never forgotten…

This book is dedicated to Rose and Jennifer, two very inspirational ladies whom I have had the honour of working alongside as a team (the best team), and we grew to become the best of friends. These two amazing ladies taught me very early on about the importance of good quality care standards, and to stand up for people's rights to be treated with dignity and respect.

Rose and Jennifer gave me the freedom and creativity to strive to be the best activities coordinator I could possibly be. They gave me the opportunity to train and work within specialist dementia care.

To them I owe my loyalty and my gratitude always.

I thank you sincerely,

Clare x

.

CONTENTS

ACKNOWLEDGMENTS

Thank you from Clare...

This book is the result of many years' worth of research, training, and experience working within the health and social care sector. It would not have been possible without the immense amount of information and experiences that I have gathered over the years – including conversations with many individuals at all levels from care home managers, carers, health care practitioners, domestic staff, residents, patients, their friends and of course activity coordinators.

A very special thanks to all of the patients, their families and residents within residential care who have opened up their doors and sometimes their hearts and without whose true-life stories I could not written this book or had the inspiration to stand up for people's rights and choices and in doing so promote and champion dignity in care.

A big thank you to all the people who have helped to make this book happen.

Thank you to our families for giving us unconditional love and support and for believing in us.

Thank you to my husband Tony and our 3 children for being so understanding and supportive to give me the time to write this book.

Thank you to Mr Vinod Taylor DL for always inspiring me to be a kind human being and sharing your wisdom and support always.

Thank you to Jennifer Taylor for your guidance, friendship and professionalism in teaching me to stand up for what's right in life and to champion dignity within care.

Thank you to DVG Star for making this book possible, your kindness and support has been amazing.

Thank you to Dr. Joan Bailey MBE, you have always been a role model to me and I would like to personally thank you for the opportunities that you have given me over the years.

Thank you to my nan - Ms Maureen Hammond MBE for being my inspiration in life to be the strong independent woman that I am.

Thank you to my dear friend Kelly Campbell – Director of Waymayka Ltd, for always being there to give me guidance and a listening ear and for the many giggles we have together.

Lastly – thank you to Rigerta for putting up with my crazy ideas at all times of the day or night, for always making me laugh often in the unexpected moments and for always being by my side in all that we do.

Thank you from Rigerta...

I would like to start off by thanking my brave and courageous Royal Humane Society award winning business partner and dearest friend Clare, this book would not be possible without you and your drive to always help and support everyone; nothing is ever too much trouble and you are always there for us all. We will make a positive difference in this world one step at a time, I can promise you that.

Thank you to my amazing family for always motivating me and continuing to support our dreams for Meaningful Education, I am so proud to be your daughter and your sister. Lastly, the one person who I feel deserves to be here with the heroes above, Jensila Avdyli – you are my pillar of support and you never fail to show me unconditional love.

We would both like to thank Sharon, Josh and all of our friends by choice service users, our students and colleagues who have continued to support our vision, mission, projects and services at Meaningful Education Ltd. CIC.

.

FOREWORD

I am deeply touched and honoured to have been asked to write this forward. I have spent over 40 years working with people both young and old who are society's most vulnerable and victimised. I have questioned so many times the strategies and action plans that have been designed by authorities to engage with and support these individuals and groups. What I have come to realise is that there is a real mismatch between the rhetoric of many social issues and the reality. We are inundated with so much academia but not so many offerings for those of us working at the grass roots level to guide us on what works for our clients.

The services we offer for older people are essential to enabling them to have the best quality of life that they deserve for the rest of their lives. The reality is that many do not get this service because the complex needs of older people are not always fully understood. This book is particularly relevant to all those who take care of others because if we understand that caring role, we are more likely to deliver care with the needs of the person at the core.

I welcome this book by my colleague Clare, who has utilised her personal experience of working in the care industry to share the reality of what this work really entails, the challenges that must be faced and the frustrations that nearly tear you apart. She talks about her work in supporting people with multi-faceted issues, including dementia and mental health problems. In doing this work she highlights the importance of treating people with care and with dignity. They seem like two very simple words that can be delivered with little thought; however, the reality is that we can only achieve these things with our clients if we invest the That is the focus of this book.

Clare highlights her working career and how these words have become the focus of what she strives to ensure happens in all interactions she has with others. By supporting people on an individual basis and delivering work using a person-centred approach, she has ensured that we look deeper into their personal needs, provide them with specific care and treat them in a way that they can retain their self-respect.

The benefits of this book are of huge importance in enabling the reader to consider a range of practical actions that can be undertaken that allow this caring role to be delivered using a more focussed and significant method. This means moving from delivering care in an unthinking, robotic way which can be thoughtless and mechanical to one were every action is considered and well thought-out. This moment by moment thinking allows us to stop and consider what is best for the client and ultimately if it is in the client's best interest.

This stop and think approach will result in what Clare advocates in her book as treating people with dignity. If we stop to consider the self-worth of people when working with them, we are more likely to think about their physical and psychological needs, the actions we need to deliver in order to retain their self-respect, and to ultimately to build their self-esteem.

I have been party to many sessions that Clare has delivered to colleagues and students about dignity and the role we need to take on in our service delivery to champion this essential element of our work. What I have taken away from these events is the core principle that Clare advocates in relation to dignity: It is a basic human right, not an optional extra. This means that it is an integral role when caring for others and should form the basis of what we do for them.

Clare encourages us to adopt dignity as an all-embracing part of what we do in our work, which means ensuring that other people also understand their role in giving the best to clients. It also means challenging organisations and individuals by speaking up about services and challenging behaviour to influence and inform colleagues, and acting as a good role model.

This book is a breath of fresh air, personal and thoughtful, giving the reader an insight into how some of Clare's personal experiences have forced her to question how we treat others and have driven her to embark on a lifetime commitment to highlight and promote the essential ingredients of dignity. She encourages us to become good role models and champion the need to treat people with respect, particularly those who are less able to stand up for themselves.

I hope that, like me, you will embrace the importance of this book in becoming a Dignity Champion and acting, no matter how small, to ensure that people are treated with thought and compassion, because kindness matters.

Dr Joan Bailey MBE

CHAPTER 1
CLIMBING THE LADDER

It was the month of May 2015 and I was meeting Clare for the first time, through a mutual friend who had asked me if I wanted to join them on a new venture they had plans for. I was not all too sure of what the plain entailed; I will be honest, I did not understand at the time but I knew that Clare was passionate and I was ready to do something I have always wanted to do, and that was to help people. Whilst in university I discovered that my interpreting was not going to suffice as experience for my marketing and advertising degree, therefore I started my search for a suitable volunteering role where I could gain experience but also give back to the community. It all started when The Alzheimer's Society (the Alzheimer's Society is a United Kingdom care and research charity for people with dementia and their carers) were advertising for many roles at the time and one of them was to join them on the media team. I was very excited and it was local, within Luton town centre, and the hours were reasonable as I could work around my university schedule.

It was a lovely sunny afternoon around June 2013, and I had been invited for an interview, my first volunteer position interview. I tried to find the location using my maps, which estimated that it was about a five-minute walk from the mall shopping centre and this was correct, but I did not know the area very well, so I got lost. I thought, 'Great, this is not the first impression I wanted for this role'. I eventually found the place and made my way upstairs, where I was greeted by a member of staff. The lady was one of the coordinators at The Alzheimer's Society and she was undertaking all of the volunteer interviews. I will be very honest and tell you that I did not know what The Alzheimer's Society was or what they did, however, the lady reassured me that I would be involved no matter what as they offered training to all volunteers. The interview started and I was given the unfortunate news that a volunteering role within the media team was not available and that the majority of the media roles were based at the headquarters in London. She offered me the role of 'Information Support' and explained what the roles and responsibilities were, making sure that I was going to be involved in event organising and stall hosting. This was amazing news because this was going to be relevant to my degree and being an information support volunteer meant that I had to make contact with potential clients and present the information in ways that they would benefit from it. This was marketing and I couldn't be happier!

During my time at the society, I found myself more and more involved in the other services that they offered, and my university studies would come to an end each year by June. This granted me extra time to learn about dementia, attend conferences and plan other events that were due to take place. I was grateful for the experience and opportunities as I was exposed to many different things that I wouldn't have otherwise experienced, I witnessed the vulnerability of people, the struggles that carers faced, and the need for services and support within the community. My colleague at the society had told me about an amazing woman called Clare and how she wanted me to meet her because she had a proposal for me. I was excited yet very nervous at the same time. My colleague was calm and wouldn't tell me everything as she knew the information would be best delivered passionately and enthusiastically by Clare. I remember a knock on the door and a voice saying, 'Hello my darling' with a tone of excitement. Mind you, this has been Clare's signature greeting for as long as I can remember whenever she enters a room. I was shy and taken back by all the emotions, and with a drink in our hands the meeting started.

The initial proposal from Clare was for me to be the marketing manager for the business and develop a marketing strategy, and this was so exciting. My initial thoughts were 'How am I going to do this?' and 'Will I be able to do this?' I had spent the last three years at university studying marketing and advertising, preparing for this moment. August 2015 was the month Clare and I started developing our vision to form a community interest company, and this is when Meaningful Education CIC was created. Starting a business at the age of 22 was scary. I look back to that moment and think, 'I wish I could give you some advice', however, I believe different experiences in life prepare you for the bigger events that are due to take place. Throughout the last four years, we have had some of the best times and, reality be, some of the worst. But where else do you have the freedom to help people, implement out of the box ideas, and do all of this with an amazing business partner?

Our signature courses, as many people are aware, are based on health and social care, mental health, and dignity. In 2016 we received our first ever cheque from the Greggs Foundation community scheme to undertake a free course for unpaid carers. This course was funded and available to carers in the community. This was my first experience with our famous course 'Meaningful Daily Activities (MDA)'. As an organisation we make sure that all our staff experience the different training courses we have available, in order to understand our true set of values at Meaningful Education. I joined the four-week course to understand what I was going to be marketing; I felt this was important for me to connect with our target audience and create a rapport with them. I did not understand why activities played such an important role not only in a professional care setting but also in our everyday lives, as children's activities are a big part of us growing and developing certain areas of our brain, and this is just as important in our later years as we grow older. Clare is a fantastic facilitator when it comes to our Meaningful Daily Activities course; the passion, care, and knowledge that she incorporates into the learning environment not only makes for great activity coordinators but gives peace of mind to the carers looking after their loved ones day in, day out.

I continued to attend all of the courses run by Meaningful Education when we first started, as mentioned before this was mainly to understand what I was to be marketing to our target audience. However, as our delivery was on demand for the Meaningful Daily Activities, we were called to places such as High Wycombe and Hemel Hempstead. I will never forget the day when Clare and I drove to High Wycombe; we had an idea of where this was located within the UK but had never been there before. We decided to leave early that freezing December morning as we knew it was rush hour and we would most likely get stuck in traffic. The morning was cold and bitter, the air had a crisp, ice-cold smell to it that sent shivers up your body the minute you stepped outside your door. It was foggy, and Clare and I were making our way on to the M25 (London Orbital Motorway that encircles almost all of Greater London). There was a truck in front of us indicating to take the exit to High Wycombe; its wheels were spewing dirt onto Clare's windshield and she had to act quick as it was starting to block her vision. She paused and looked at me with a grin and said 'I have run out of screen wash'. Then she said calmly 'Look behind your seat and you'll find a big water bottle', I quickly took the bottle and waited patiently for the next move, which I believed would be Clare pulling over. This though was not the case. Laughing, Clare said, 'Now open the window and throw some water on the windscreen'. I couldn't get my words out due to how much I was laughing. (I did not do this by the way, just for your peace of mind. We are safe drivers.) We did laugh so much that day.

Clare and I finally arrived in High Wycombe, even with the screen wash situation and don't let me forget roundabouts on roundabouts; nevertheless the roundabouts are a story for another day.

On arrival, we realised that parking was going to be difficult and if we parked farther from the location, we would be late for our first session. We had to make a good first impression as this was an important course booking for us. I took all the materials in our 'trolley' and went to find the training room we were going to be teaching in, so that I could prepare everything for the lesson to start. I was extremely nervous, and Clare's phone had run out of battery and was now turned off and I didn't have any indication of when she was coming back or if she had secured parking. I walked into the room that was booked for us, only to realise that it was full of our students, waiting for us to begin our session. My heart was pounding as I said 'Good morning' and introduced myself to everyone. You could hear the trembling in my voice. Without realising, I babbled on with extra information they probably didn't want to know, and this was all due to the fact that I was nervous and waiting for Clare to arrive at any minute to take over. I soon realised that maybe parking was harder to secure as I did not see Clare walking in with her superwoman outfit on. I had to do something to save our first impression, so I quickly eased them into their first activity where they all could get to know each other better, a little ice breaker to get started. Halfway through this activity I heard Clare walking in through the door saying, 'Good morning everybody'. I don't think she will ever forget the look of relief on my face. The course ran smoothly, and everyone seemed to have enjoyed the day. As we were packing the activities away, I remember one of the learners approached us and said 'Thank you for being the most inclusive tutors I have ever met, you made me feel comfortable and spoke to me with nothing but respect'.

I will never forget that day and the positive impact we had on our learners. This was my first official involvement in facilitating our Meaningful Daily Activities course and what was the beginning of our programmes and projects that Bedfordshire had never seen before.

I observed the way that MDA ran as a course for a long time before I took the scary step of facilitating one completely by myself. In 2017 I qualified for an award in education and training, which was originally known as PTLLS. Without this it was not going to be possible for me to facilitate any of the Meaningful Education (M.E) courses. If you have worked with us or know of our work, you know that it can get very demanding. My favourite M.E course has always been and always will be Understanding Mental Health; for me it is one of the most interesting courses to facilitate as we adapt it for different organisations and community groups. The feedback that we receive on this course makes you realise the different experiences that people have had throughout their lives, whether that be in their professional role or in their personal lives. We were busy at M.E as we were now running community services as well as designing and developing training programmes for facilitating courses.

Clare asked me if I could facilitate an MDA course over at The Hub, which is where our office is based. Clare was booked to teach at a carers' academy, facilitating the Care Act Standards course. We had some very interesting people in attendance from neighbouring boroughs and counties. I was very nervous as I had only ever seen the MDA course run in the last couple of years and never actually facilitated this course by myself.

I walked in to our training room at The Hub that morning

and Clare was already setting everything up for me. She did not want me to be nervous for my first and official course alone, and we went through a lot of the materials and she kept reassuring me by reminding me that 'It will be okay, you know all of this already'. I did know all of the materials on the slides and I understood the activities very well, but I was still very nervous. I kept thinking to myself 'What if I mess this up?', 'What if I ruin this experience for the learners because I have not got the relevant experience in the activities world?' My thoughts took over for a bit and at this point I was scared; scared of being judged, and these thoughts and feelings took over at that moment and I would have done anything to get rid of that feeling. Whilst lost in my own thoughts, our office bell rang: My learners were here for their 4-week course. Without thinking I quickly made my way to reception to greet them and walk them through to the training room. They walked in and picked their seats and settled themselves, and I kept telling myself 'I wish I had more time' because the nerves were still there. I directed the learners over to the kitchen in the building and kindly suggested they make a cup of coffee or tea before we began. This again was a tactic to give myself more time. More time for what, you may be thinking? At this point I was unsure myself because the nerves had taken over. I looked over the lesson plan again whilst the students got their tea and coffee, and as I saw them making their way back to the training room I told myself stop thinking about this so much and just get on with it, Rigerta.

The course ran smoothly for the next four weeks and I genuinely cannot tell you how happy I was. I knew it was going to be okay but the nerves kicked in as I did not want to disappoint the learners who had paid to come to our course. In many ways I am a perfectionist, and this has held me back in completing a lot of things within the timelines that I set. I see a certain vision of how perfect something can be and I know my own set of skills in order to do this. I expect nothing less than this, and this is why I get nervous when facilitating as I want to give the learners the best version of myself, the best materials, and I want them to walk away knowing that they are confident in themselves to deliver once they are back in their care setting. Our core aim at Meaningful Education when Clare and I first started was that we concentrated on providing the most holistic and inclusive training that motivated and empowered our learners, and to equip them with the skills, tools and knowledge to best prepare them for the care settings in which they are to work in. We expect nothing less than this. I have since continued to facilitate on all courses at our organisation, and throughout the years I have always said that I lack experience compared to the vast amount of industry knowledge and experience that Clare has.

But Clare has always been so supportive and taught me that life is full of experiences and that we develop and grow personally and professionally every day, and that these experiences will naturally be reflected upon over time. We pull on our learnt knowledge and experiences, often referencing these within our training delivery to give an example of real-life experiences. I can honestly tell you that as I sit here writing this chapter, I could never have anticipated or imagined the extent and diversity of the experiences and opportunities that I was going to work in. The knowledge and skills that I have since developed is beyond my hopes and dreams, from starting our own community interest company, to developing community services to meet the demand and need for mental health support within the community, to being requested to be practitioners to support the victims of the tragic Grenfell Tower fire and being part of the crisis intervention team, to then being invited to participate in the green paper discussions at the House of Commons, and visiting Parliament.

To conclude on my experience throughout the last couple

of years, I found it difficult to adapt in the beginning as I did not quite understand why activities played such an important role within the care of an individual. From a basic understanding I knew that children learn through play and it 'allows children to use their creativity while developing their imagination, dexterity, and physical, cognitive, and emotional strength. Play is important to healthy brain development', as stated by Kenneth R. Ginsburg and the Committee on Communications, and the Committee on Psychosocial Aspects of Child and Family Health, 2007. This is also important as our brain starts to age; it is recommended by some doctors and scientist that as we get older we need to keep our brain active by learning a language, playing Sudoku, and other brain training games that are now accessible through our phones and tablets. Activities are another avenue for adults as well as children to explore, and as an activity coordinator you have a very important role, as Clare will explain at lengths in her chapter. You are responsible for the growth and continued development of the people within your care, and I say this lightly as I do not want anybody to panic, but your role is very important as activities are a focal point in helping to support a person living with dementia. A recent research study from UCLA as explained by brainhq.com, 2019, says that

'Exercise stimulates the brain plasticity by stimulating growth of new connections between cells in a wide array of important cortical areas of the brain'. They demonstrated 'that exercise increased growth factors in the brain – making it easier for the brain to grow new neuronal connections'.

Without going to deep into the psychological benefits in this chapter, I wanted to highlight the similarities between brain development in the early years of our lives and as our brain develops as we grow older. Clare discusses the importance of being an activity coordinator and what it takes to be one, and in the following chapters we will look at the different core needs of people living within care settings and how these core needs can be met. I conclude this chapter with the importance of having a healthy lifestyle and making healthy lifestyle choices: Our choices for our health and well-being will take us into our old age and we will benefit from our choices of today.

CHAPTER 2
GOING IN BLIND

I had my own business. I was a salon owner, and in addition to this I was travelling up and down the country (England) styling models' hair for fashion shows and wedding expos. It was an exciting and creative job that I really enjoyed. My work became really full on travelling and very long hours, so I decided to sell the salon as I was away more and more, and I felt I wasn't able to commit to both equally. From May to September was the busiest time within the industry - wedding season!

Everything was going great, but then it all had to change. My mum was diagnosed with breast cancer and I made the choice to be home more to support my mum through this time. I took a little time off to attend all the appointments with my mum to fully understand what treatment plan was needed and to be there to give emotional support throughout this worrying time.

I needed to work, but I couldn't carry on with my long hours working away; I needed to be flexible and to be local in case I was needed to help my mum. I started to apply for jobs locally, ones that were flexible.

One morning, I was sitting drinking my coffee and job searching when I came across a job advertising for an activities and events coordinator. The advertisement said flexible working hours and it was only a 10 minute drive from where I lived. I called the number on the advertisement and a lady answered and I explained that I was interested in the job and asked how I could go about applying. The lady said, 'I am interviewing today, can you come at 11.30am?' I looked at the clock and it was 10.05 am. I replied, 'Yes, of course, see you shortly', and then went into panic mode as I needed to change out of my jogging bottoms and t-shirt and to prepare and get there on time. In a mad rush I got ready and went along to the location at the local council where the interviews were being conducted.

I remember sitting there thinking I can do this, I have been working at events up and down the country. The job advert said experience wasn't needed but was desirable.

My name was called and off I went. I was introduced to the manager; she seemed really friendly and welcoming. She was with a staff member sitting at the desk. The interview began, and I gave my CV and my portfolio folder showing my work at events. I must say I really wasn't given much information at all and I was so nervous and younger back then (early 20s). I was told the hourly rate and that there would be training that I would need to attend, and that it was 20 hours a week which were flexible. It sounded like the perfect job! I was told I would need to set up activities and arrange entertainment and events. I thought to myself this was great; it worked for me personally as it was part time flexible hours should I be needed to attend any appointments with my mum. It was like this job was made for me!

"I received a call later that day offering me the job. I was over the moon and super pleased. I was told that I would need to visit the manager to provide some documents to complete a CRB check – The Criminal Records Bureau (CRB) and the Independent Safeguarding Authority (ISA) have merged to become the Disclosure and Barring Service (DBS). CRB checks are now called DBS checks.

Which enables employers to make safer recruitment decisions and prevent unsuitable people from working with vulnerable groups, including children. DBS checks the Police National Computer for details of all current criminal convictions." (Criminal Records Services; 2019)

At that point I didn't even know what CRB / DBS was! I sent in my references and documents as requested and my DBS was approved, and I received the call to confirm my start day.

I remember thinking, I don't even know what the company does exactly or who their client base is. I was so naive back then! I was given the address of the company to attend my first day at work. I remember arriving and looking at the building thinking 'This looks like a house.' I was expecting a corporate looking building. I rang the doorbell and I was greeted by the staff member who was at the interview. She showed me into a lounge where I waited to be called to see the manager. I remember thinking it looks like what I would imagine to be a care home. Well didn't I hit the nail on the head! I was about to start my activities job in a dementia care home! I'll be very honest; I didn't even know what dementia was back then! I kind of had an idea; I thought it was something we get when we get old - forgetfulness!

Looking back now with my many years' experience, if I had known the full job requirements and job description would I have applied for the job? Probably not, because I lacked the knowledge to understand it. So, I can sit here and say yes, my naivety and lack of understanding led me to this job, but it has been one of the best opportunities and the best decisions I have made. It happened for a reason. It was meant to be!

I met with the manager and I was given an introduction

and shown around the building. I was then introduced to my deputy manager - Jennifer. My first impressions of Jennifer, she was very professional and a little scary as she came across quite strict. (Sorry Jen!)

I was shown to a room where there was a desk and what looked like a storeroom. I was told to go through the activities and pick something to do with the residents and I was left to it. I remember thinking this was not the job I thought I applied for and what on earth am I going to do?

So, I thought, you know what, Clare? Make the most of it and get on with it, it can't be that hard, right? How wrong was I!

I picked up a puzzle and a dart board- it had magnetic darts which looked quite good.

I walked towards the main lounge, and there was a lady walking up and down the corridor repeatedly calling out '546713, 546713, 546713.' I said hello to her but it was like she didn't see me and continued on her walk repeating these numbers over and over again. As I arrived in the main lounge area, I looked around: There was a lady (resident) sitting playing the piano and singing *Roll Out the Barrel* and some residents were singing along. It was a really lovely atmosphere and made me smile.

I always loved the older generations and love listening to their stories and experiences. This love came from many wonderful summer holidays spent with my grandparents in London and being around their friends who were all elderly.

I approached a gentleman sitting at a table by himself, and I went over and introduced myself and I asked if I could sit next to him at the table. He replied, 'Yes, of course.' I told him it was my first day there and would he like to do this jigsaw puzzle with me? He replied, 'Yes, why not?' And so I began placing all the pieces on the table, and we began chatting away together as we did the puzzle. I noticed that his hands were shaking a lot, and his responses were slow. It reminded me of when I was a little girl and I used to visit my grandad. I remember my mum telling me that my grandad had Parkinson's disease and as I was only around 8 or 9 years old at the time when she told me, I never really fully understood what that meant, so I just thought Parkinson's meant you get the shakes! The gentleman had a Scottish accent; he was kind and friendly which helped to ease my nervousness, and we seemed to of connected well. He was called by the carer who told him that the doctor had arrived to see him. As the gentlemen got up, he said to me, 'Thank you, you're a lovely girl, I'll see you around,' and off he went.

I packed the puzzle away and off I went to see if anyone else would like to do the puzzle or play darts. As I walked into the conservatory area, the sun was beaming in and it was rather hot. There were around 4 or 5 residents sitting in this warm and cosy area. I noticed a man sitting facing the sun, he was wearing sunglasses and was smiling, facing the warm beams of the sun, and he was humming away happily. I walked over to him and said hello and he turned towards me and said hello back and then faced the sun again. I explained that I was the new activities coordinator and introduced myself. I asked the gentleman if he would like to play darts with me. He replied, 'Yeah alright then, that will be lovely.' I placed the felt darts board in front of him, hanging it on the wall, and I passed him the darts. He began throwing them in all directions, and I had to dodge a few! A carer came walking over and she didn't look impressed with me! 'You do know he's blind, right?' At that point I wanted the ground to open up and swallow me whole! I felt so awful. I had just asked this gentleman to play darts and he couldn't see the darts board. But I wasn't to know, no one had told me he was blind and had dementia. The way he had interacted with me gave me no indication of this. I apologised profusely to both the gentleman and the carer. I felt at that point that I wasn't even going to last the day at this rate! On reflection now, the carer's reaction and what she said openly in front of the gentleman, the residents and the staff was not dignified. Yes I was inexperienced and uneducated within this sector at that point but now with training, knowledge and many years' experience I can sit here and say that all activities can be offered to all if you adapt to the individuals' needs and abilities, making activities accessible and inclusive for all in a person-centred approach.

I managed to get through the rest of the day without upsetting anyone else and spent the rest of the afternoon talking to and getting to know the ladies and gentlemen (residents) within the care home. That night when I was at home reflecting on my day I just felt so awful, I never wanted to offend anyone. I mention this to you as this was a big learning curve for me that contributed to shaping my professional career, as I have never forgotten this moment. From that moment on, I made sure that I read all patient or resident files and care plans where possible to do so, to ensure that I KNEW each and every person I was there to support. I took the time to meet and talk to all residents, their families and staff to learn about how I could best support each individual and how to meet their needs, wishes, choices and preferences to enable a meaningful daily life through stimulating and engaging activities.

I wanted to make sure that I enabled all residents to participate in all activities and I learnt very quickly how to adapt activities to each individual's needs, abilities, choices and preferences, always adapting to ensure inclusivity. This was a huge learning curve for me. I massively underestimated the extent and diversity of this role and I often had to think outside of the box and delve deep to be as creative and innovative as I possibly could.

Looking back to my interview day, when I was told I would need to attend training, I can now tell you that since then, I have attended many training and educational courses and workshops. Rose (the boss) used to enrol and sign me up for too many, often 2 or 3 courses at a time! Yes I used to moan, but I have always remembered Rose saying to me, 'My girl, you listen to me: You study and you take every opportunity that comes your way. You're young, so get as much under your belt as you possibly can, because it will open up doors for you later in life.' Rose pushed me to work hard and mark my words, I have worked so hard over the years and I still continue to do so. Rose was right in what she said, and I have taken on her advice and the opportunities when they have presented themselves. I have never stopped learning to this day! In fact, this is something I have always instilled in Rigerta, and pushed her to learn and grow in her professional capacity. And when I look at the opportunities I have opened up to Rigerta, and the opportunities that she has created herself, it is tremendous to see where she started to where she is now. Her knowledge and experiences that she has achieved all by the age of 26 years old is phenomenal!

We can all create opportunities to learn and grow as an individual both personally and professionally, but it also comes down to the person, their qualities, experiences, personality and their goals in life.

I have always been a hard-working person, with great empathy, compassion, and a caring nature towards others. I have always observed situations in life with a strong mindset that if it were me, how would I want to be treated? Or how would I want my family members to be treated? It's an easy answer: with dignity, kindness, compassion, understanding and a listening ear! So, I always try to treat people this way and to make people feel that they are important and to help and support as fully as I am able to do so.

So, yes, I survived to tell the tale of my first day and how I got into working within dementia care as an activity coordinator.

CHAPTER 3
THE UNSUNG HEROES OF HEALTH AND SOCIAL CARE

Being an activity coordinator can be one of the most rewarding and fulfilling roles; it can bring so much joy, happiness, fulfilment and well-being to both the service users/residents and the activities coordinators, but at times it can also be quite an isolating role too.

In terms of staffing ratio, there is quite often only one activity coordinator working within the care setting and you are often expected to provide all of the engaging and stimulating activities, entertainment and events to ALL residents/patients varying from 1 - 70 plus service users or maybe even many more, compared to the average ratio of 1 carer per 6 residents/patients! As a coordinator, you have to be able to work on your own initiative and to be very self-motivated within your role while being able to motivate your service users, their families and colleagues to participate in the daily activities. Have you ever heard of the phrase 'jack of all trades, master of none?' Well, that's kind of how I felt. The ideology of an activity coordinator is to know how to do everything and facilitate a diverse range of sessions like being a teacher without actually being a trained teacher, to be an artist and to facilitate a range of creative art and crafts sessions, to be a historian and to know how to delve into centuries of historical moments to create many engaging and stimulating reminiscence activities, to be a fitness instructor or personal trainer and to be able to facilitate physical exercise activities, and the list goes on and on.

Your role may include: talking to residents to find out about the types of activities they'd like to take part in and organising the many diverse activities tailored to meet the complex needs and abilities of the many individuals you are there to support, as well as providing group activities that will bring individuals together to provide a social interactive experience, while also assisting people in taking part in activities by visiting those who are in their own personal rooms. Being an activities coordinator is one of the most diverse and multi-functional roles to work in.

What I loved about being a coordinator was to see that I had enabled a smile or to hear the laughter that I had brought to so many that day, creating an environment of happiness and joy to those that I am there to encourage and support. It is wonderful to be able to see that you are connecting families to spend quality time with their loved ones, while having a listening ear for those wishing to share their memories and experiences with you as they provide a window into their world through meaningful and engaging conversations, and providing a sense of purpose and self-worth to their day.

I remember a carer once saying to me, you are here to do your job, not get connected to residents. Well let me tell you this, when you are supporting many individuals on a daily basis who are quite often vulnerable, unwell physically and mentally, or are receiving palliative care, you get to know each individual's preferences, what they like and don't like, what makes them smile and be happy, what may upset someone, you learn their behaviours and their communication preferences and how to preserve and respect their dignity.

As a carer or activity coordinator, you will spend on average 8 to 12 hours per day with these individuals, day in, day out, for months or maybe even years. These individuals become like your extended family members. It is not like working in a hospital where patients are admitted and discharged with quite a fast turnaround. I would hope that when choosing your career to become a healthcare professional, like a carer or a coordinator, that you do so for the right reasons: because you want to help and support people, because you care! To care, to have empathy, kindness and compassion is an intrinsic emotional process, and it does not always come naturally to everyone. Because you care about the individuals you are supporting does not mean you are being unprofessional, it means you have the right qualities for the profession. After all, the proof is in the pudding as they say, and they don't refer to the 'care industry' as the 'we don't care industry!' I became an activities coordinator and I have worked as a carer and a care manager, and I can honestly and genuinely say that it was because I care about each individual's health and well-being, their dignity, and their daily living is of the utmost importance and I am there to be of service and support them as fully as I am able to do so, both professionally and empathetically. Remember, if you are working in a care home setting, this is someone's home, their home where they live with their personal belongings, so always be respectful of that. Over the years, unfortunately, I have seen many care professionals who portray the mindset that the residents are in their place of work, creating a divide and misunderstanding of the environment in which they work. This creates barriers and can lead to institutionalised practice.

Becoming a healthcare professional is not an easy role to facilitate in any way shape or form - far from it. There are many struggles too, like the mountain of paperwork you have to complete at the end of each day, writing up the daily records on each individual and stating who participated in what activities, how they appeared during the activities, what their feedback was, how their interaction was and so forth.

So, imagine writing up a whole day's worth of activities for each individual for 40 to 80 residents or more! It is a VERY time-consuming daily task and can take a few hours to complete depending on the number of residents you support. If you're an activities coordinator reading this, then I am sure that you can relate!

I have taught many activities coordinators over the years and this is always one of the frustrating struggles and topics of discussion during the workshop. It is your responsibility as a professional coordinator that your records are considered extremely important and will be referred to as a recorded document. These documents are often viewed during external and internal inspections to check the standard of care and support within your setting, and other health care professionals may seek to examine the individuals' daily living when assessing their needs and health care plan. So, the daily records are an important responsibility, one that is a major requirement of the job.

As an activity coordinator there is a reason and a purpose in all that we do. Activities provide a sense of purpose to a person's day, and can provide some enrichment to their daily living, but with all the best will in the world, sometimes it just doesn't always go to plan and you have to think on your feet, adapting to the diversity and complexity of dementia. It is draining and tiring, and sometimes there is a lack of support from care staff to help because they are busy too, and it can be like pulling teeth out just to play a game of bingo! But, I enjoy it and it is fun and rewarding, and by the end of the day when I've talked so much that when I get home I'm all talked out and physically exhausted from running around playing balloon tennis and I've completed over 1,500 steps on my Fitbit. I can finally sit down and breathe!

There was often a misconception, or some may say a 'running joke,' that all I did was mess about with glitter and paints and sat chatting, which wasn't seen as working, as I would often get told. If only everyone understood how hard coordinators work and how hard it is to make it look easy! One thing I did implement in one of my care homes that I worked in was that all staff had to learn and swap roles with other members of staff on a training day. This challenged misconceptions and changed mind-sets and taught valuable lessons in respecting all roles and responsibilities within the care setting, as each and every person working within the setting is vital to the professional facilitation of the daily practice. It provided a sense of respect for all roles and responsibilities and to appreciate the value of teamwork. This was conducted with all members of staff from the chief and kitchen staff, domestic staff, maintenance and care staff and of course activities staff. Walking a day in someone else's shoes provides an insight into understanding their role and responsibilities and how hard these roles are to facilitate. I also provided dignity awareness training for all staff. This is something that I am strongly passionate about, as one day I watched a carer approach a man who was sight-impaired, sitting at a dining table, and he had finished his dinner and was sitting alone. As the carer approached him, she said, 'Hello, you've finished your dinner. Come with me to the lounge' and she took him by the arm and led him to the lounge where he sat in a chair and she walked away. I remember thinking, if it was me how would I feel in that situation?

I thought about it a lot that day and even that night, and if it was me that the carer had approached, would I have liked to have been treated that way? I felt there was a lack of communication, a lack of choice, and a lack of dignity. The next day I went and spoke to my manager and voiced my concerns and opinions, to which she said, 'Well, Clare, teach the staff to understand dignity'. My manager knew how much I championed dignity and how passionate I am about treating people with dignity, and so I went away and thought about it.

A few days later I had a plan! I was going to ask the staff to become residents for the day! Over the course of a week I chose 2 carers a day who agreed to fully participate and to role play for the duration of the day their assigned medical diagnosis. We bandaged up one carer's legs and restricted her mobility, which created a unique insight into what someone may experience due to their medical conditions.

The carer that I had previously seen lead the gentleman who was blind to the chair, well there was no question about it, she was to have her vision restricted for the day. So we covered her eyes with patches. This experimental dignity training was perfect and achieved the desired outcome that I had hoped for. The blind carer was asking repeatedly 'Where am I? What am I near? I need help. What's in front of me?'

Did she explain the surroundings to the gentleman when she moved him from the table to the armchair? No, she did not! Did she give him choices on where he would like to sit? No, she did not! The carer took those choices away by placing the gentleman in the armchair without explaining his surroundings, what he was near, who was close by and so forth. At the end of the day we sat and reflected on the day and discussed how the carers felt, what their experience was like for them individually and how it made the care staff feel. It was a great learning experience, an insightful activity that challenged their mind-sets and provided a deeper awareness and empathy that brought dignity to the forefront of their minds and actions. It was clear in the weeks after the training, when I observed the staff's conduct, that it was evident that there were big changes in terms of communication! The interaction between staff and service users was much more dignified, more respectful and more choices were provided.

In fact, we went one step further and all staff were to promote and become dignity champions! We signed up for the dignity in care campaign, led by the National Dignity

Council. All staff became dignity champions, and we implemented a champion of the month incentive, whereby once a month we chose a member of staff who had shown best practice in their duties, someone who went above and beyond to champion dignity and their name would go up on the staff notice board in bold as the champion of the month and they would receive a certificate and flowers or chocolates for being such a great role model. The National Dignity Council exists to shape and influence the work of the dignity in care campaign, and also campaigns for and supports dignity champions. I have always held the National Dignity Council with such high regard, and the values that they promote was where a lot of my inspiration comes from. I wanted to be a dignity champion and wanted to promote it and shout it from the rooftops! I wanted to always make sure that I had the best intentions at heart, to always try to be a kind, caring human being and to challenge any poor practice or disrespectful behaviours. I have always wanted to make a positive difference in this world, and I hope that little by little with dignity, kindness and compassion that I can bring a little bit of happiness to those around me. In the words of Mahatma Gandhi, 'Be the change you wish to see in the world'.

I have been a dignity champion for many years now, and I am proud to promote this in all that I do. "To be a dignity champion is to promote the core values of having dignity in our hearts, minds and actions." (Dignity in care; 2019)

"You can become a dignity champion by joining the many thousands who have signed up for the dignity in care campaign. The campaign's core values are about having dignity in our hearts, minds and actions, changing the culture of care services and placing emphasis on improving the quality of the care and the experience of citizens using services, including NHS hospitals, community services, care homes and home services." (Dignity in care; 2019)

CHAPTER 4
CORE NEEDS

When getting to know the individual interests and preferences of all the residents, it is important that there is effective communication in understanding their choices.

As we begin to understand what drives our decisions and behaviours on a daily basis, we can then develop an awareness of why we do the things that we do.

By understanding the individual interests and choices, this will enable you to develop a well-structured activities program, one that is tailored to the needs and abilities of every resident within your care setting. It is also important to find out and assess what activities are suitable.

In my teaching capacity, I often ask coordinators how they plan their activity programs, and it is said that searching on google or Pinterest for ideas is a main source of inspiration. This is good if you have done your homework first, and what I mean by that is that when planning activities, it always needs to be person-centred to meet a person's core needs.

When I first started as an activity coordinator, I'll be very honest, it was trial and error to see what worked and what didn't by providing a range of different activities (often with limited resources) and listening to the residents' feedback on who enjoyed the activity and who did not and what the experience was like for them. I spent a lot of time, months even, getting to know every individual and often spent many hours of my own time doing lots of life history research, documenting my findings to build a comprehensive life history of each individual where I was able to do so. I then started to develop this further by creating individual activity-focused well-being plans. I felt that in order for me to provide a meaningful daily living to those that I was there to support, I had to know how to improve a person's well-being physically, mentally, emotionally, socially and spiritually.

"While each of us is unique and shaped by our individual life events and corresponding emotions, we also share behavioural systems that generally function in the same way. Tony Robbins has discovered through over 40 years of experience that there are 6 human needs that fundamentally affect the way we make choices. Each of us prioritise our needs differently, and our decisions are based on which needs we put first." (Tony Robbins Blog; 2019)

"Robbins's theory is that there are 6 human needs, which he believes are:

1. Certainty: Assurance you can avoid pain and gain pleasure
2. Uncertainty/Variety: The need for the unknown, change, new stimuli
3. Significance: Feeling unique, important, special or needed
4. Connection/Love: A strong feeling of closeness or union with someone or something
5. Growth: An expansion of capacity, capability or understanding
6. Contribution: A sense of service and focus on helping, giving to and supporting others"

(Tony Robbins Blog; 2019)

Although I agree with this theory to some degree, I do however feel that as a professional working within health and social care, and to be more specific specialist dementia care, I spent many years tailoring activities to meet the core needs of dementia patients. Don't get me wrong, I am not merely implying that a diagnosis of dementia means that the core needs differ, but what I did identify over many years of directly supporting these individuals was that there is a commonality between us all, which in my opinion is the desire for 'fulfilment', a 'wholeness'. These needs are not merely wants or desires but profound needs and form the basis of every choice that we make. Many of our behaviours are based on which of our needs are – or are not – being met. Depending on which basic core need is of more significance at the time, you could be spending a lot of time consciously or subconsciously trying to meet one or two of them. And if you are unsuccessful, it could negatively impact your overall sense of well-being. When a core need is unfulfilled, it can impact your ability to connect with others, and it could also cause a change in your emotions and influence your mental health.

In the past, people were expected to fit in with the routines and practices that health and social care services felt were most appropriate. But in order to be person-centred, services have changed to be more adaptable to meet individual needs in a manner that is best for them. This involves working with individuals and their families to find the best way to provide their care and to provide a meaningful daily living. This partnership work can occur on a one-to-one basis, where individual people take part in decisions about their daily living, health and care, or on a collective group basis whereby the public or patient groups are involved in decisions about the design and delivery of services.

Person-centred planning is about considering people's

desires, values, family situations, social circumstances and lifestyles; seeing the person as an individual and working together to develop an appropriate activity plan, one that will enrich a person's daily living. It is also about being compassionate, thinking about things from the person's point of view and being respectful.

When creating an activities plan, it is fundamental that you take a person-centred approach to meet the individual core needs.

Below are the 10 core needs to focus on when identifying how to plan the activities.

1. Faith, religion, beliefs, spirituality
2. Culture
3. Emotional
4. Physical
5. Social / community interaction
6. Creative
7. Learning / development / intellect
8. Sensory
9. Self esteem
10. Dignity

By using the 10 core needs model as a guide, explore with the individual, and their families where possible, their life history, their hobbies, interests, likes, dislikes, careers, education, social interaction – clubs, groups attended, etc. Once you have identified these you will then gain a comprehensive understanding of the person's life history, which will enable you to map suitable activities to meet the individual's core needs.

So, going back to my original question 'How do you plan activities?' one would now say 'I plan all the activities taking a person-centred approach, based on their life history and choices to meet the core needs of the individuals that I support'.

For example, I remember being in a staff hand-over meeting when I was informed of a patient who would be arriving later that day from hospital. Sadly, he had been in hospital because he had a stroke and had been diagnosed with Alzheimer's dementia. I was told that the gentleman's mobility was very limited, as was his speech, and that he required a lot of support. Later that day, the gentleman arrived, and I introduced myself to him. I was there to help and support him with the transition from hospital into the residential care, as this can be a very confusing time and is sometimes a little scary too when in unfamiliar surroundings. Over the first few weeks I spent a lot of time getting to know him and providing support for this gentleman. We had many great conversations and I remember him telling me about living in Spain for over 25 years. He described his villa and spoke fondly of his neighbours and of the Spanish culture that he had adopted and loved for so many years. This gave me an insight into the fond memories that he cherished so dearly and gave me ideas on creating engaging activities that would be of interest to him. He also spoke about his love for photography. He went on to tell me that he had been a pilot in the RAF (Royal Air Force) during WWII and how he used to fly the spitfire aircrafts and take aerial photographs using the built in reconnaissance camera which was used to obtain intelligence about the enemy and their activities. He showed me old photos that he had taken of various places that he had visited during his time within the RAF.

We talked about many things over the weeks, and it was during these discussions that he shared his frustration in relation to losing his mobility and how it had impacted on his dignity and independence. I could see this meant a lot to him, and so over a period of several weeks we explored his aspirations, hobbies, interests and what dignity meant to him and how I and the care team could support and preserve his dignity. I worked with him to create a person-centred activity plan, and what was clear was that he wanted to improve his mobility in order to regain a better quality of independence. We spoke to the health care team and assessed his health care needs. This was a man who could barely mobilize independently and required full assistance when moving physically. Through a robust activities plan, we (the gentleman, care team and I) set aside dedicated time each day to work on physical exercise activities, starting with very low-level impact exercise to begin with, increasing over time and assessing regularly. Over time, this plan enabled a better well-being; in fact, I can tell you that this was a man who needed full support to stand from being seated via the support of a handling belt. Nine months later, I can honestly say that through a dedicated activity plan and setting daily goals, I had to physically run after this man when we used to go out and take photographs of nature and the countryside views as he was walking unaided again. With a lot of hard work, determination, support and consistency, we were able to rebuild and rehabilitate this man's mobility and independence. It also had a very positive impact on his mental well-being.

These experiences I share with you identify the value and meaning that activities have in enriching a person's daily living. Every person you support is an individual, and so not all activities are going to be suitable for everyone. I cannot stress enough the importance of understanding and knowing the person and their life history, as it is of the utmost importance before planning any activity. One thing you would hope to avoid is that even with all the best intentions, you don't want to offer an activity that could potentially be a trigger that could cause harm or upset to an individual.

Documentation is always a time-consuming affair, and as you can imagine creating a person-centred activity plan for each and every resident will indeed be a very time-consuming task! However, this can be added to your activities program as a valuable one-to-one activity, engaging in a meaningful conversation, one that has a reminiscence element to it. As a coordinator, I created a robust system of evidence-based practice. As we all know, inspection ratings are extremely important to the success and viability of your care setting. There is increasing awareness and focus on the daily activities that are being provided and there is no question that registering authorities are paying increased attention to the quality and the individuality of activities being provided and offered to service users.

"The Care Quality Commission (CQC) regulates all health and social care services in England. The commission ensures the quality and safety of care in hospitals, dentists, ambulances, and care homes, and the care given in people's own homes." (Gov.uk; 2019)

All care homes are required to conform to a set of standards. These standards can be found on the CQC website. CQC monitor care homes and conduct regular inspections – at least one 'review' every two years. It also takes in feedback and concerns from residents and those who have loved ones in care home.

If like me you are utterly dedicated, enthusiastic and highly motivated within your role, then fully embrace the unannounced inspections as a positive! I was always proud of the achievements that we as care providers had accomplished. I wanted to show the great meaningful work that we did to support those within the residential home. I couldn't wait to demonstrate the engaging and stimulating activities that were being provided on a daily basis. I wanted to show how activities were having a positive impact on the residents' well-being physically, mentally, emotionally and socially.

I have had the honour and privilege of working in some of

the most amazing care settings with outstanding staff who work with such care and compassion, and I have sadly seen some care providers who do not, which is often why you would see the panic on their faces when they were informed that the inspectors had arrived to carry out their observations for the duration of the day. But rest assure there are MANY amazing care providers with dedicated caring staff who have the utmost professionalism, kindness and compassion. We need to shine a light on these health care heroes who are working extremely long hours, and this is by no means an easy career choice!

CHAPTER 5
5 WAYS TO WELL-BEING

We hear the word "well-being" a lot, but what does it mean? There has been a lot of emphasis on looking after the well-being of others in the previous chapters, but it is also equally important to look after your own well-being too!

"One in four people in the UK will have a mental health problem at some point. While mental health problems are common, most are mild, tend to be short-term and are normally successfully treated, with medication, by a GP." (Health and Safety Executive: 2019)

"Mental health is about how we think, feel and behave. Anxiety and depression are the most common mental health problems. They are often a reaction to a difficult life event, such as bereavement, but can also be caused by work-related issues." (Health and Safety Executive: 2019)

As a health care professional you may be required to work long hours in a highly demanding role, which can also be a daily emotional roller coaster, so it is paramount that you identify your needs and how you can proactively look after your well-being, physically and mentally.

There are two main elements to well-being: Feeling good and functioning well.

To feel and function better, there are things that you can

do to improve and maintain your own healthy well-being.

A recent government-commissioned study revealed that three times more people lose their jobs due to poor mental health rather than physical health every year. With aging populations, cost inflation and tight budget constraints on national health spending, the government is looking towards companies to fill the gaps in provisions. More than simply a widespread personal problem, it's fast becoming a major public health, employee well-being, and business issue.

"Work-related risk factors for health"

"There are many risk factors for mental health that may be present in the working environment. Most risks relate to interactions between type of work, the organizational and managerial environment, the skills and competencies of employees, and the support available for employees to carry out their work. For example, a person may have the skills to complete tasks, but they may have too few resources to do what is required, or there may be unsupportive managerial or organizational practices. Some jobs may carry a higher personal risk than others (e.g. first responders and humanitarian workers), which can have an impact on mental health and be a cause of symptoms of mental disorders or lead to the harmful use of alcohol or psychoactive drugs. Risk may be increased in situations where there is a lack of team cohesion or social support." (World Health Organization; 2019)

"Creating a healthy workplace"

"An important element of achieving a healthy workplace is the development of governmental legislation, strategies and polices as highlighted by the European Union Compass work in this area. A healthy workplace can be described as one where workers and managers actively contribute to the working environment by promoting and protecting the health, safety and well-being of all employees. An academic report from 2014 suggests that interventions should take a 3-pronged approach:

- Protect mental health by reducing work–related risk factors.
- Promote mental health by developing the positive aspects of work and the strengths of employees.
- Address mental health problems regardless of cause."

(World Health Organization; 2019)

There have been many occasions over the years, where I have been in employment, clock watching, thinking is it 5 o'clock yet? And many times, where my alarm goes off in the morning and as I awake my stomach would feel with dread and negative emotions at the thought of having to go into work! These are common signs that we need to acknowledge and pay special attention to look after our own well-being.

Employers are becoming more proactive in bringing wellbeing to forefront of the workplace culture. It is imperative to consider when constructing wellbeing initiatives to take a holistic approach that focuses on the following elements:

- ➢ **Physical**
- ➢ **Social**
- ➢ **Mental**

Especially mental and social health, because ignoring one of them will not address well-being appropriately.

Here are some examples of how companies may address these 3 parts;

- Free Gym Memberships for employees – Physical exercise is great for your Physical and mental health.
- Counselling – This is a proactive way to support an employee in their recovery.
- Mindfulness sessions – A great workplace incentive to take part in during lunch breaks or at the start of the working day.
- Workplace peer support group

These examples above have many additional benefits such as building confidence and self-esteem, decreasing social isolation and increasing social interaction, and can be used as self-help strategies outside of work too.

Let's look at ways to improve well-being at work

Here are a few suggestions you can do to improve physical, social and mental well-being in the workplace.

1. Take the Office Outside

Pick up your laptop and get outside! Sit in the local park, field or roof top terrace. Get some fresh air, and feel the warm sun beaming down on your face as you work in beautiful surroundings. We have a lovely big open space of land by our offices and on sunny days we get out the office and into the fresh air and it's quite lovely!

2. Carpool Meetings

An absolute favourite of mine! Okay, so as a director of a community interest company, time management is often a struggle! It was during a time when Rigerta and myself were working days and nights that we began having our meetings in the car when driving back and forth between London and Bedfordshire. We had some of the best discussions, and we used our time effectively! Win, win! We even went on to create a playlist of songs and would often sing a song or two between topics of discussion! Who ever said work meetings can't be fun? It's time to get creative! Plus, singing and laughter are GREAT for your mental well-being!

3. Walking Meetings

"Walk and Talk" meetings or lunchtime walking groups are a proactive way to improve your well-being - physically, mentally and socially. And it's completely FREE!

4. Well-Being Days

A great way to increase social well-being is by arranging team building days! Encourage different teams and departments to come together, creating a more collaborative working environment.

Example:

- Carers & Admin staff - Bowling tournament
- HR & Domestic staff - GO-Karting
- Maintenance team & Courier drivers - Golf tournament.

I think you get the point we are trying to make here!

5. Team Sports

"A study of 1.2 million people in the USA has found that people who exercise report having 1.5 fewer days of poor mental health a month, compared to people who do not exercise. The study found that team sports, cycling, aerobics and going to the gym are associated with the biggest reductions, according to the largest observational study of its kind." (Science Daily; 2019)

6. Technology Activities

Technology is widely accessed by many these days, from smart phones to iPads, tablets, and gaming devices. You could consider setting up challenges across departments or across the whole company! Here are some examples:

Words App With Friends – An interactive and engaging online game where you compete against each other.

Fitness challenge – Which employee can complete the greatest number of steps within that week or month? (Smart phones / Fitbits / smart watches are a great tool for tracking your steps!)

Guess the song – There are plenty of apps available across all devices and you could pick a different theme or era each week.

Kindle book club – Each month a different employee gets to choose a book for everyone to read and at the end of the month you all meet to review / feedback.

There are many wonderful incentives you can put into place at and it doesn't have to break the bank either!

As activity coordinators, carers, health and social care staff working within care settings (care homes, hospitals, day centres, community centres, etc.) or if you are caring for a loved one or family member at home, it can be an exhausting process, mentally and physically. Burnout and compassion fatigue are terms carers regularly hear when caring for someone with a mental illness.

Caring and supporting others can take a serious toll on carers' mental and physical health, their personal relationships and family finances. Without the support they need, this can lead to carers' collapsing due to exhaustion, suffering physical injury or becoming overwhelmed by stress and anxiety.

Common symptoms of exhaustion

- You can't think straight – or even think at all
- You are more than just a 'little' stressed out
- Physical exhaustion, where you feel tired most of the time and are unable to complete tasks to the same standard you once did
- Your usual healthy snacks have been replaced by chocolate bars, crisps or just carbs in general and gallons of wine
- Changes in appetite, or losing your appetite all together
- Frequent headaches and tension
- Using alcohol or drugs to cope
- You find yourself unable to fall asleep or stay asleep
- Your lips are constantly cracked and dry
- You can't bear the thought of the gym
- Loss of motivation
- Feeling helpless
- Your mood is dark and stormy
- Social withdrawal
- You feel short of breath – even when you're doing nothing at all
- You seem to permanently pick up the office cold – having a lower immunity resulting in frequent sickness / days off work
- Your sofa and PJs are your new BFFs

Many of these symptoms are also experienced in a

depressive episode and can feel just as overwhelming. If you feel you are experiencing these symptoms, it's important to act now and prevent the effects of burnout from becoming even more consuming or devastating. As stated by the "NHS, and various other health care professionals, there are "5 recommended ways to achieve your overall well-being." (NHS – 5 Ways to wellbeing; 2019)

These are:

1. Connect
2. Be Active
3. Give
4. Keep Learning
5. Take Notice

Rigerta and I looked at the 5 ways to well-being, but what does it mean? And how do you implement this into your daily living? So, we decided to take on the "5 ways to well-being" by doing a "5-day challenge" and each day we would take part in and try out a diverse range of activities to meet each of the recommended 5 ways to well-being. But for our well-being week of challenges we also decided to add "Time for ME" as this is something many of us lack in our daily living.

On searching the internet to learn ways in which we could achieve our well-being goals, we found many lovely diagrams for well-being that gave the recommended headings, as stated above, but what do they mean, exactly?

I am a little lazy when it comes to exercise, I'm not going to lie, but if the truth be told, it's because I work very long hours and quite often 6 days a week. I know this is no excuse, but really, the last thing on my mind is to sprint round the local park at 7pm at night or hit the gym after a 12-hour shift! Having said this, I am fully aware that I am clearly not looking after my own well-being as best as I can and should, hence why I accepted the challenge!

Slow and steady wins the race, as they say!

Starting off slowly, I wanted to ease myself in gently. When it comes to physical ways to stay healthy, the gym, Pilates, Yoga, Zumba, and spin classes get all the attention when it comes to popular activities! There is, however, a more unassuming workout that doesn't quite seem to catch the attention it so rightly deserves!

Walking! What I love and have learned (remember Keep Learning is No. 4.) about walking is that pretty much everyone can do it - at any age and at any fitness level. This is very much an activity that you can adapt to your own personal ability levels. You don't need to be Usain Bolt! Plus, it is good for your heart, your mind and your wallet too!

It was a beautiful sunny warm day, and myself and Rigerta set out to begin our well-being walk. I'll be honest, it really did not seem majorly appealing to me, but I was open minded to try, so that's a start, right?! What I didn't anticipate was how much I was going to thoroughly love it, and the breath-taking landscapes and scenery that I had the privilege to see! This was a benefit, as I would not have had the opportunity to see the beautiful scenes if I was driving.

First stop was a nature trail within Hertfordshire. It was a lovely big open space with quirky little hidden treasures! It was lovely to be in the fresh air, with the warm sun beaming down. I work a lot within an office environment, and this also includes a lot of travelling across London, Hertfordshire and Bedfordshire. It is a fast-paced daily life, with busy traffic, tubes, trains and lots of interaction continuously, so this beautiful walk in peaceful and calming surroundings was just what I needed for my own well-being. A sense of calm! And, it's not until you step out of your "normal" environment and reflect, that you see and feel the benefits, and the importance of taking time out to look after your own well-being.

Moving on we then went and visited another breath-taking country-side location – Sundon Hills, in Bedfordshire. It was stunning! There was a nature trail there too, and a lovely heard of sheep to keep us company on our walk! The spectacular views and big open landscapes were mesmerising! It really was a complete mental and physical well-being workout! And, what was even better is that I had completely lost track of time (I am always working to schedules and appointments - clock watching) and we had walked for over 45 minutes and it didn't even feel like a strenuous workout, bonus! And, if you want to take it to another level like I did, I also incorporated photography as an additional "add on" activity. I love photography, and this has become quite a lovely little hobby for me. I love to take photographs of beautiful scenery and of course capture those great moments spending time connecting with friends and family (remember Connect is No.1 and Take Notice is No.5). Your well-being really doesn't have to cost a penny if you don't want to spend a penny, and by us completing this well-being walk, we completed 4 of our recommended well-being challenges: Connect, Take Notice, Be Active and Keep Learning.

This stimulated our minds and was a great physical workout, and we connected emotionally, as friends, with nature, making memories and of course stimulating those lovely feel good hormones – endorphins – in the brain!

Over the week we took part in many activities from eating healthy, to volunteering (Give is No.3) to reading and learning, and we discovered new activities and new things to do in our local area that we were previously unaware of. On our travels, keeping on the theme of staying active we embarked on trying out HotPod Yoga!

HotPod Yoga classes offer a 'real-life' approach to hot yoga in a completely otherworldly setting. Refreshing and impactful, the classes have roots in vinyasa flow and are grounded firmly in reality – whether you're there to work off a hangover, clear an over-stimulated mind or open-up an office-bound body, HotPod Yoga delivers – guaranteeing to leave you with a (slightly sweaty) smile on your face as you emerge from the pod.

Rigerta and I attended a class taking place in Crownhill - Milton Keynes. HotPod Yoga is suitable for most levels of fitness whether you're a beginner, professional, young, elderly, male or female! (Always remember to seek prior professional medical advice before taking part in new physical activities.)

We only needed to bring water and a towel with us to enjoy the unique immersion of the HotPod. The pod itself is a beautiful, cocoon-like, pop-up, inflatable, heated studio and comfortably accommodates 20 people inside. "This inflatable pod is heated to 37 degrees to supercharge the yoga experience." "We completed sequences of active and passive postures to ensure a balanced physical workout while also allowing space and depth to calm the mind. The 37-degree heat and ambiance melts you deeper into your practice by warming muscles and aiding flexibility while the Hot Pod yoga teacher guided us through a flow of postures that opened up our bodies, worked our hearts and calmed our minds in equal "measure." (Hotpod Yoga: 2019)

Once completed we left with our minds a little calmer; our bodies a little looser, and yes – we were a whole lot sweatier!

So remember, as wonderful as you are for caring and supporting others, please do be mindful that you are just as important and it is a MUST to look after your own well-being too.

CHAPTER 6
CORE NEED:
RELIGION, SPIRITUALITY AND
CULTURE

Today, we live in a world in which we are fortunate enough to be in the presence of many different cultures and religions. I use the word fortunate because there was a time when people had no access to on-demand information and content from around the globe and migration was not as easily accessible like it is today. We now live in a world where you do not have to travel to another country to understand different cultures or religions; immigration over the last 60+ years has welcomed different foods, fashion and an understanding of a diverse way of living. Technology, as mentioned above, has given us unlimited accessibility to information from different countries across the world, all at one time and across a range of different social media platforms. In this chapter I will begin by defining the difference between religion and culture, whilst looking into the core need aspects, and the importance this has in your care setting once you have a greater understanding.

People are quick to judge when it concerns an area or a topic which they have limited knowledge on. When seeking information and greater knowledge on topics we do not understand, we are quick to source this information from platforms that are quickly accessible. Yes, we may be fortunate to have access the way we do with technology, however, it can be just as damaging as it is beneficial when sharing information across the internet. Social media platforms have features such as #hashtags, tags, quick story updates, and technology that allows you to go live wherever you are. The information that is accessible out there is sometimes manipulated by famous news channels, entertainment magazines, and media outlets who want stories and features in order to make money, therefore creating ideologies and stigmas towards certain religions and cultures, which the majority of the time are incorrect.

As defined by (Lexico, 2019) Oxford dictionary:

Culture: "The ideas, customs, and social behaviour of a particular people or society."

Religion: "The belief in and worship of a superhuman controlling power, especially a personal God or gods."

To understand the difference between the two you will need to understand some important factors that make up culture and religion. Culture is the social heritage of every individual who is from a particular society. Hofstede, 1994, states that "Culture is the collective programming of the mind which distinguishes the members of one group or category of people from another". People from the same cultural background will recognise people from the same country/heritage as them. I have personally been fortunate to have been exposed to different cultures whilst living in Luton for the last 18 years. There are many different communities within Luton and you have the opportunity to not only learn about different cultures but also have a taste into their food, music and traditional customs through restaurants, events and community open days. I always say to Clare that I can recognise a person from my own Montenegrin/Albanian heritage, and when saying this I am referring to their accent, the way in which they carry themselves and the activities that they might participate in within the community. I am able to say this because I am from the same background, and because of the particular society we come from, we live a certain way of life that almost mirrors one another.

In times of uncertainty people will turn to what they have faith in, and for a lot of people this will be their religion. This helps people understand misfortunes that they may be going through and that are happening around them. In order to act appropriately or carry themselves in a certain way in all situations, people gravitate towards moral conduct that is heavily influenced by their sacred texts in the form of scriptures and books. Within religion they worship God/gods, making faith the backbone of many societies. In times of difficulty people can be divided by religion, even when they are from the same society/culture. There is an old saying in Albania, 'Albanian first'. This is because they have mixed religious beliefs, some more devout than others. In times of uncertainty Albania is reminded that they are Albanian first before anything else and they need to look after each other based on the fact that they share the same cultural background, regardless of religious beliefs.

It is difficult to define the true difference between culture and religion as the majority of the world has the two intertwined and they are heavily influenced by one another. However, recently I was watching an interview by David Letterman with Malala Yousafzai (a young activist for the education of young girls). They were discussing the precepts that her culture stands by, which are hospitality and asylum that are instilled in the moral code of Pashtun culture (Afghanistan, known as ethnic Afghans). Malala highlighted that people are welcome in the homes of Pashtun without an invite and that they are allowed to stay for as long as they want without feeling unwelcome. There is another factor which I would like to highlight in this section, and it is a little negative compared to the example from of the young activist

Malala. Religion is used as a method of restriction in South Asian countries and Arab nations. An example of this is in 2017, King Salman of Saudi Arabia "ordered that women be allowed access to government services such as education and healthcare without the need of consent from a guardian" (Independent, 2017). In 2018, women were finally allowed to drive, and it is quite alarming to think how many women have suffered throughout the centuries due to a lack of independence. In locations such as South Asia and the Arab nations, the Islamic religion is used to restrict the freedom of women, therefore creating negative preconceptions, when in reality Islam promotes the opposite.

This topic has many factors, but my discussion here will give you a basic understanding of the background of cultures and religions, which will have a big influence on the activities you implement into your care setting and for the person whom you are caring for. Within this chapter we will look at Christianity, Islam and Hinduism, being the three religions that have the largest number of followers in the world. Below I have included the basic understandings of the three religions as defined by Lexico (2019) and Dictionary.com (2019):

1. **Islam:** "The religious faith of Muslims, based on the words and religious system founded by the prophet Muhammad and taught by the Koran, the basic principle of which is absolute submission to a unique and personal god, Allah."

2. **Christianity:** "The religion based on the person and teachings of Jesus Christ, or its beliefs and practices."

3. **Hinduism:** "A major religious and cultural tradition of South Asia, which developed from Vedic religion...sharing a belief in reincarnation and

involving the worship of one or more of a large pantheon of gods and goddesses."

This section will concentrate on the activities you can incorporate into a care setting in order to involve residents, loved ones and staff members to understand and enjoy the cultural and religious celebrations that take place throughout the year.

What you can do in your care setting

There are many activities you can implement throughout the year within your care setting to make the environment inclusive for the residents and their loved ones. In order to have a better understanding of the cultural and religious days that do take place throughout the year, I recommend creating a calendar where the most important days / dates are marked. Below I have listed in relation to religion the different activities that can take place for the most sacred days:

1. Islam

> **Ramadan:** Muslims spend a month fasting during the daytime. This is normally done "corresponding with the ninth month of the lunar calendar" (Learn Religions, 2019). From sunrise to sunset, Muslims abstain from food, water, sex and smoking. However, what should be noted is that people are excluded from fasting if they take medication, are pregnant or are on their menstrual period.

In order to celebrate Ramadan you can provide different meals from around the world throughout the month of Ramadan as Islam is practiced across every country in the world. During this time, Muslims give out food to their neighbours and volunteer in order to build on their good deeds. Creating relationships with different community groups, organisations and businesses will give you an advantage as you can invite them into host activities in which highlight who they are and what they do.

> **Eid:** This day is the celebration of the end of Ramadan, which is normally celebrated by breaking your fast with your loved ones and then attending Eid prayer in a mosque or an outdoor area hosted by local communities. This will be a great time within your care setting to invite family members to your facility for a celebration day, and provide food and activities for children and the whole family to enjoy. Hiring a photographer for the day who creates a range of different creative scenarios would be a great incentive to create memories.

> **Everyday inclusion:** As a Muslim you are obliged to participate in the 5 daily prayers that take place during the different hours of the day, 'Fajr' prayer being at dawn and 'Isha'a' is the night prayer. The timings can be found on the internet and are always by the area in which you live or at your local Mosque. Take the same concept here as the calendar and create an activity where you set daily/weekly/monthly reminders of the prayer times in a fun, interactive way. It is always beneficial to have a prayer room and Quran available to make them feel at home. When purchasing food/ingredients, it is important to ensure that it is Halal (permissible) "the Islamic form of slaughtering animals or poultry, dhabiha, involved killing through a cut to the jugular vein, carotid artery and windpipe" (BBC News, 2014).

This is very important to remember as the majority of foods may not be permissible.

2. Christianity

As mentioned above, Christianity is based on the teachings of Jesus Christ. It is believed by Christians that Jesus Christ is the Son of God, being born in Bethlehem in the Middle East thousands of years ago. Similar to Islam, Christians believe that there is only one God: "Christians believe that God sent Jesus to live as a human being in order to save humanity from the consequences of its sins – the bad things humanity has chosen to do which had separated them from God" (BBC, 2019). In every religion, there is an element of sacrifice and it is believed in the teachings of Christianity that Jesus Christ was sent to earth by God, being his only son, in order to restore the broken relationship that were created between God and the people of the earth. What you need to be mindful of and do a little bit of background research on when it comes to Christianity is the new and old testaments, and this is where the new testament will be mentioned (known as 'the Resurrection'). This is important as you will have a better understanding of the fundamental beliefs of the people within your care environment, therefore adapting your daily activities to their needs holistically.

Christmas

Activities may include
- Watching the Queen's speech on Christmas Day, particularly if an individual is a royalist and promotes British values.

Aim

Her Royal Highness the Queen publicly addresses the nation in her annual Christmas Day speech.

The Queen's speech is commonly known to be aired at 3pm on Christmas Day. The Queens speech is generally a reflection of the events that have taken place over the year. Her Majesty's speech tends to focus on key elements such as, The British Empire, the commonwealth of Nations and her own personal contribution, reflecting on her family and feelings at Christmas.

As an activity this is often a time that can bring people together who share and value the British culture and values. The Queens speech is an important speech where the Queen addresses the Nation. Invite family members, residents, neighbours around to watch the speech together, a great social activity. Great opportunity to create a forum for discussions after Christmas lunch. Encourage conversations about previous kings and queens and future heirs to the throne. Other activities may include a Christmas carol sing off competition! Compete over skype with other local care home providers!

Pancake Day (Shrove Tuesday)

Pancake Day is the last day before the period of Lent which leads up to Easter. It is traditional to eat pancakes on this day because they contain fat, butter and eggs which are forbidden during lent. If any of your residents are Christians, it is important to embrace this traditional day and you may want to encourage residents and their families to share memories and discuss different recipes. You may also want to consider activities around this which may include:

- Pancake making
- Pancake tasting
- Pancake flipping contest
- Pancake Bake off
- Art and crafts

Easter

Easter celebrates the resurrection of Christ and is the most important and oldest festival of the Christian Church. This event is generally held between 21 March and 25 April, on the first Sunday after the first full moon following the northern spring equinox.

This is a great time to take part in many activities from arts and crafts, to baking, with many social event's cross communities, schools and churches. The Easter themed activities to choose from are long and endless, giving so much choice and diversity, for example:

- Easter egg hunts,
- Arts and crafts
- Easter egg decorating
- Easter bonnet making – fashion hat paraded/ competition
- Easter quiz
- Parties
- Fates
- Sunday services
- Spring themed photography
- Nature trails
- Easter card making

Ash Wednesday

"Each year, Ash Wednesday marks the beginning of Lent. Often called the Day of Ashes, Ash Wednesday starts Lent by focusing the Christian's heart on repentance and prayer, usually through personal and communal confession." (Christianity.com: 2019)

"Each year, Ash Wednesday marks the beginning of Lent and is always 46 days before Easter Sunday. Lent is a 40-day season (not counting Sundays) marked by repentance, fasting, reflection, and ultimately celebration. The 40-day period represents Christ's time of temptation in the wilderness, where he fasted and where Satan tempted him. Lent asks believers to set aside a time each year for similar fasting, marking an intentional season of focus on Christ's life, ministry, sacrifice, and resurrection."
(Christianity.com: 2019)

Activities:
- Bible reading
- Trip to your local church
- Invite the local priest or minister to conduct an informal service within your care setting.

Also consider celebrations and activities that will support the following:

- Sunday church service
- Christian hymns – music activity
- TV – songs of praise
- St David's Day
- St George's Day
- St Patrick's Day
- Christmas Eve
- Christmas Day
- Boxing Day
- Birthdays

3. <u>Hinduism</u>

Diwali

"Deepawali, Deepavali, or Diwali is the biggest and the brightest of all Hindu festivals. It is the festival of lights: *deep* means "light" and *avali* "a row" to become "a row of lights." Diwali is marked by four days of celebration, which literally illuminates the country with its brilliance and dazzles people with its joy." (Learnreligions.com: 2019)

"The Diwali festival occurs in late October or early November. It falls on the 15th day of the Hindu month of Kartik, so it varies every year. Each of the four days in the festival of Diwali is marked with a different tradition. What remains constant is the celebration of life, its enjoyment, and a sense of goodness." (Learnreligions.com: 2019)

Activity ideas:
- Invite people from the local Hindu community to come and visit your care setting and speak about the festival.
- Listen to Indian songs.
- Display pictures of the Hindu gods and have a discussion about each god.
- Encourage residents who are Hindu to speak about aspects of the Hindu religion.
- Create paintings, colour in pictures of the gods to display within the home.
- Create cards to give to the community.
- Make lanterns.

Different religions have their very own commemorative days that are sacred to the faith of different societies and though they cannot be changed, an individual's religion can be included in their everyday care in a lot of ways.

I always find adding all the awareness days and cultural celebrations events to the calendar at the beginning of the year helps me to plan ahead! If you are unsure of the dates you may want to check out https://www.awarenessdays.com/ which I have always found to be a useful resource.

CHAPTER 7
CORE NEED: CREATIVE AND
SENSORY ACTIVITIES

Creativity is and has always been explored in different ways. When you think of creativity you most likely think of arts and crafts, art pieces in a gallery, spray paint murals and even activities which allow you to create different pieces of art through sketch books, canvases and guided painting through numbers and selected colours. Psychology Today (2019) interprets creativity in a different way by looking at psychology: "While research psychologists are interested in tapping innovating thinking, clinical psychologists sometimes encourage patients to use artistic expression as a way to confront difficult feelings". We go back to children's play for a moment, as art is a way of expression for children and this allows them the space to express their feelings and ideas. Have you ever wondered how that is so? As mentioned, art is normally seen as an activity, for example to keep your children occupied whilst you get on with the housework or whilst travelling. Penn State Extension (2019) states that children do not need to have a finished product as they "use paints, glue, and markers, children are planning, trying out new things, and solving problems. As children mix paints, they learn to understand one thing can make changes in another" allowing them to make their own choices through play. Sensory activities are also very important for people to understand. They play a really big part in stimulating sight, touch and hearing within individuals. Through this we learn to discover new sensations which will allow us to not only create but also explore our different senses.

We briefly understand from the first paragraph to why creativity and sensory activities are important in our general development, but you're probably asking, what about in our care settings? In the next section we are going to look at the most important aspects and how you can relate and adapt them to your care environment so that your clients/residents benefit from them and have an improved quality of life.

Sensory activities have been used for a very long time in care services by activity coordinators to allow residents/clients to explore and engage their senses in the most creative ways. The methods used can be really powerful for the people that are affected and are limited by their cognitive abilities. It can really be as simple as looking through old photographs or playing cards. Creativity plays a huge part in the sensory activities as it can be the make or break factor when creating sensory activities. An example for this can be non-toxic paint which not only washes off easily but allows clients to paint with their hands or feet to feel the different textures, as well as the wonderful colours that they can create.

Another great activity is aqua paints! We have used these many times, and can enable service users to feel confident in their creative abilities by the support and vibrant colours that aqua paints provide.

Why is sensory stimulation so important?

The care environment is becoming more established when it comes to planning and designing sensory activities for residents/clients. Sensory stimulation includes many benefits such as an improvement of mood, and an encouragement of relaxation and reminiscence (Abbeyfield, 2019). There are many activities which include sensory stimulation that are recommended, such as learning a new language, gardening, yoga, etc. There are many recommendations when you think about sensory stimulation and we will look at what that looks like briefly in the next section so that you have a better understanding, allowing you to incorporate your own ideas when planning, designing, and creating new activities.

Global Council on Brain Health (2017) wrote a handbook on 'Recommendations on Cognitively Stimulating Activities', with writers from professions such as policy writers, health professionals, and scholars. As the Global Council on Brain Health they have managed to concentrate on 'brain health relating to people's ability to think and reason as they age'. Within their research handbook they focus on cognitively stimulating activities, however, what will be most beneficial to you is the recommendations in which they discuss people living with dementia. The following recommendations are discussed (please note for the full version you can find the reference at the back of the book):

1. Engaging in routine activities that associate with daily living, i.e. making their bed, helping with the washing, and setting the table for meals.

2. Self-care, everyday involvement, i.e. brushing their teeth, doing their hair, getting dressed in their choice of clothing (please note this all based on the individual and their ability at the time of care).

3. Engagement in setting up activities such as music and craft sessions.

4. Group sessions that involves the individuals taking part in discussions, i.e. they can create discussion cards relating back to their years of growing up.

5. Social engagement - it is important that they are involved in activities that they enjoy and find interesting, i.e. meeting new people. This will be beneficial as they have to learn their names and new information relating to this person.

When looking after a loved one or working within a care setting, Global Council on Brain Health (2017) states that "it is also important for caregivers themselves to keep engaged in cognitively stimulating activities." This is so that you look after your own mental well-being. There are many sources and articles that will be beneficial as a care provider to explore; as we say at Meaningful Education, 'early intervention is the long term prevention'. Taking this factor into consideration, in your role you must aim to create a multi-sensory environment in order for the people in your care to not only fully engage but to have the opportunity to grow as an individual. A great example of this is Clare's story about the older gentleman who was not able to physically engage in activities, however once the right stimulating environment was put into place, Clare was running after him! Rhino UK (2018) interprets this well by concluding that "time spent in a multi-sensory environment has been proven to increase concentration, improve motor skills, creativity, social relations and communication and general awareness of the surrounding world". Our brains have the ability to react to external factors and also to the changes that may occur within our own bodies, even in our old age. Taking what we have learned from multiple sources into consideration, we will be looking at an experience below which hopefully will give you the additional motivation to explore some of the readings in our reference list.

It was January 2017, a very cold January, and myself and Clare were on our way to Hemel Hempstead to introduce our brand new MDA (Meaningful Daily Activities) two-day intensive course to new recruits at a housing association. It was all very exciting for me as we adapted this course to the needs of the clients that the housing association catered to. However, in order to do this, we invited one of our colleagues along to facilitate one of the days with us. The specific day in which we facilitated together was concentrated on clientele with limited mobility, vision, and hearing. This was especially difficult as we had to make sure that the materials were relevant and met the needs of the staff on training. Throughout the day our colleague who had a background in limited mobility services facilitated some of the activities in which staff members had to take part. The activities throughout the two-day course explored the different aspects they had to incorporate in order to provide the right care for their clientele, and for some of the activities they were asked to tackle them in pairs and groups. This worked really well because when they had partaken in the activity, they had to then present to the rest of the group their findings in terms of difficulty and how they would adapt it to their activities on a daily basis. They discovered that one activity is not always suitable for all. In this chapter we have discussed why it is important to keep our brain stimulated, because as we age our ability to do many things starts to deteriorate and it is important to keep looking after ourselves through activities that will keep our brains active.

CHAPTER 8
A PRACTICAL GUIDE TO
MEANINGFUL ACTIVITIES

There are many activities that you can do; the list is long and endless. Let's take a look at some examples:

1. Sensory Relaxation

Residents with Dementia can often feel confused and anxious, and the nature of the disease can mean they experience episodes of aggression. By encouraging stimulating and relaxing activities, this can help to decrease such emotions and behaviours, having a positive impact on the person's overall wellbeing.

Aromatherapy is a pleasurable method of invigorating and exercising the senses and memory of your residents.

Another great sensory activity to try, is the Smell and connect cards by Reminiscent! Available on Amazon or via their website. Discover smell power with your residents. A fun and engaging activity where you can explore the 6 cards per pack, with a range of diverse scents.

"The sense of smell is the most immediate and emotional of the senses; rooted in the parts of the brain responsible for evoking memory and emotion. Whether positive or negative, this exchange results in a connection that makes a difference to how people feel about themselves, their situation and their relationships.

With this in mind, ReminiScent Ltd launched an innovative range of Smell & Connect cards, which have been designed to 'reach people through scents' and engage those living with Alzheimer's disease and dementia in conversation and activities." (homecare.co.uk: 2019)

Smelling is an act that evokes a reaction and starts an exchange of feelings or ideas. This exchange results in the human connection that makes a difference to how people feel about themselves, their situation, their relationships with carers, family or health-care professionals.

The smell and connect starter pack consists of six distinctive smells: * Tomato Plants * Victoria Sponge * Fresh Laundry * Fresh Cut Grass * Baby Powder * Chocolate Orange. There are two cards of each smell included and, by resealing the 'smell stickers' correctly, each card can be used many times over. There is one conversation card per scent.

It is extremely important to ask the person you are caring for what they would like to do first before suggesting any of the activities that are planned, remember everyone has a choice. Always make sure you have a good understanding of a person's life history as best as you are able to do so, as you would want to avoid any upset or negative triggers.

2. Breathing Exercises

This is a good place to start for anyone who's feeling anxious or stressed about their memory loss or dementia symptoms. If you start to notice that a resident / service user is becoming panicked, doing some simple breathing exercises may help to calm them.

This simple but effective breathing activity is easily accessible to do anywhere for example, from sitting in the armchair, standing up, lying in bed, at any time. Below is an example stated by the NHS. (NHS.UK: 2019)

"Make yourself as comfortable as you can. If you can, loosen any clothes that restrict your breathing.

If you're lying down, place your arms a little bit away from your sides, with the palms up. Let your legs be straight or bend your knees so your feet are flat on the floor.

If you're sitting, place your arms on the chair arms.

If you're sitting or standing, place both feet flat on the ground. Whatever position you're in, place your feet roughly hip-width apart.

- Let your breath flow as deep down into your belly as is comfortable, without forcing it.
- Try breathing in through your nose and out through your mouth.
- Breathe in gently and regularly. Some people find it helpful to count steadily from 1 to 5. You may not be able to reach 5 at first.
- Then, without pausing or holding your breath, let it flow out gently, counting from 1 to 5 again, if you find this helpful.
- Keep doing this for 3 to 5 minutes." (NHS.UK: 2019)

Doing this for 10 minutes a day or whenever they feel stressed can help to increase calmness.

3. Visualisation

"Visualization is a cognitive tool accessing imagination to realize all aspects of an object, action or outcome. This may include recreating a mental sensory experience of sound, sight, smell, taste, and touch." (psychologytoday.com: 2019)

"In psychological practice, visualization is often used to mentally rehearse an action or bring a patient to a state of relaxation. Dr. Cathryne Maciolek, a D.C. area psychotherapist, uses visualization in her clinical practice. She quotes Rosabeth Moss Kanter to illustrate the power of the technique, "A vision is not just a picture of what could be; it is an appeal to our better selves, a call to become something more." She explains that visualization is a means of control in an uncontrollable situation." (psychologytoday.com: 2019)

Visualisation is a great way to reduce stress, improve mood and boost confidence and to help a person relax the body and the mind. If you are doing this activity with someone who has been diagnosed with Dementia, I would suggest a guided visualization to support them to achieve this. Start by a few simple breathing exercises, as stated above. Then ask the person or the group to close their eyes we are going to imagine a place where you can feel relaxed and rested – for example a nice warm sunny day on a quite beach or sitting looking out over the beautiful countryside hills.

Ask each person to really focus on what they can see, smell, the colours, the way the light is shining, and sounds they may hear. Ask them to imagine what these sensations will feel like for them. Can they hear the breeze blowing through the plains of grass, or the soft sand between their toes, hearing the waves of the ocean coming and going out? How does it make them feel emotionally – happy, warm, content, relaxed, at peace?

Spend about five minutes helping them visualise this place. Then slowly encourage them to bring themselves back into the room, notice their surroundings and become aware of their body. Finally, ask them to open their eyes.

4. Mindfulness

"Mindfulness is a way of paying attention to the present moment, using techniques like meditation, breathing and yoga. It helps us become more aware of our thoughts and feelings so that, instead of being overwhelmed by them, we're better able to manage them" (MentalHealth.Org.UK: 2019)

If you use Spotify or YouTube, there are many guided mindfulness/meditations available to access. Mindfulness/meditation is a great relaxation activity. It may take a few attempts to relax as you get used to taking part in the activity but remember the environment is an important element, so ensure that you notify staff that you are facilitating this activity in order to reduce any noise levels and to avoid any interruptions. Mindfulness is an effective tool and can help to manage a person's mental health and wellbeing.

5. Magic Table

This year we attended the care show in Birmingham, where I was able to meet many different organisations from across the country, offering a variety of wonderful services, assistive technology and activities. It was during this visit that we got to experience first-hand the interactive "Magic Table" activities.

These "Magic Tables" are designed to help residents who have mid to late-stage Dementia relax and reminisce, by using the interactive light projector through simple interactive graphics and games. This technology is a great activity enabling coordinators and carers to promote stimulation through specialised games. The interactive games break through apathy by stimulating both physical and cognitive activity and encouraging social interaction.

6. A Sense of Calm

This I Love! A sense of calm is available as a DVD for or as a CD. (asenseofcalm.com: 2019)

"Sensory Relaxation works by imitating the principles of sensory rooms, by using gentle images & music the DVD can help relieve stress, anxiety and frustration. The DVD is 70 minutes long & features 7 video tracks of specially created flowing images, set to composed music".(alzproducts.co.uk: 2019)

When setting up this activity, think about creating a calming environment with low level, soothing lighting. Once the DVD is on for all to see and hear, you may want to think about offering a simple hand and arm massage which can be extremely soothing, enhancing the relaxation process. You may want to also consider the use of natural aromatherapy oils or a scented body moisturiser and use long sweeping strokes along the arm and fingers. Always remember to check before hand for any potential allergies and with a senior member of the care team before using any aromatherapy oils or scented moisturisers.

7. Reminisce About Life

"Reminiscence' means sharing life experiences, memories and stories from the past. Typically, a person with dementia is more able to recall things from many years ago than recent memories, so reminiscence draws on this strength. So many of our conversations and interactions rely on short-term memory. Reminiscence can give people with dementia a sense of competence and confidence through using a skill they still have." (Scie.org.uk: 2019)

The aim is to encourage communication and self-expression. This will also increase social interaction, feelings of belonging and togetherness through the sharing of experiences.

Activity examples:

> Looking through old photographs discussing their memories. This will not only benefit you as you will learn more about them, but it will also benefit them as they will be discussing their favourite memories.

> Group discussions - Focus on the diversity and differences of the residents within your group to obtain greater insights into each object or experience. Many Library's or local heritage centres offer services where you can hire reminiscence boxes with many different themes and different decades containing many items to look at and try. These are a good way of exploring memories and a practical activity, one that is a great talking point!

8. Cooking and Baking

Ever tried reminiscence baking? One thing I always found to be popular and enjoyable by all was reminiscence baking. This can be a fun and a productive process as there are many aspects to this that benefit all of the human senses, especially on sensory, when it comes to textures, smells, and also the different noises that are made in the kitchen.
Recalling memories through cooking and baking experiences of the past can be immensely therapeutic and enjoyable.

There are many books out there that share recipes (for example war time ration cookbooks, or cookery in the 1950's) or simply check out the endless online resources available or apps like Pinterest! Our residents loved cookery and it became a weekly activity. Residents would share their childhood memories of their favourite meals that their parents or grandparents used to cook for them when they were children. They would then go on to share their memories of their own dishes that that had created over the years loved by their children and family members. Taking this one step further we then created a "residents' cookbook" one where they shared their favourite meals and memories, and this was then created into a book form available for all to view and purchase a copy if they wished to.

Nestle UK have been "inundated with requests from carers and reminiscence groups who want historical packaging to help prompt happy memories among patients / residents diagnosed with dementia, or memory problems. Nestle have put together reminiscence packs that uses some of the most beautiful items from their archive to create a versatile, varied sensory experience. The history packs can be downloaded and printed out instantly to create a whole collection of materials from there historical archive. Links are provided within the reference page at the back of this book. The pack has been produced with advice from the UK based Alzheimer's society, which leads the fight against dementia in the UK". (Nestle.co.uk: 2019)

9. Animal Therapy

When discussing animal therapy Super Carers (2017) look at the psychological benefits by confirming that "pet therapy can help lower blood pressure and heart rate, reduce the stress hormone cortisol, and boost levels of the feel-good hormone, serotonin". There are many different organisations and projects that offer pet therapy, or you can ask a close family member or friend if they can bring their pet round when they visit. Please remember that they would have to be well behaved, and it is so important to know each individual person's care plan and health needs in order to identify any known allergies. Many schools and care homes now encourage a home pet or school pet.

10. Explore Nature

We are fortunate to have some of the most beautiful places surrounding us. Nature is practically everywhere, and it is very accessible. Explore the different parks in your area or plan a trip to the seaside. There are many different ways in which you can explore nature, you will just have to take some time out and do a little research on the internet or go for a walk in your local community to discover your environment. With the increase of technology (smart phones, iPads and cameras) why not start up a residents' photography group? Residents can go out and about in the community and take pictures which will add vibrant colour when their images are placed on display within the home.

11. Musical Activities

Music is a great form of communication and for expressing our emotions. There are many benefits to accessing musical activities and so it is no wonder that

"People with dementia are to be prescribed 'personal playlists' to alleviate symptoms thanks to a new 'Music for Dementia 2020' campaign." (ClassicFM.com: 2019)

The Campaigns Programme Director Grace Meadows states: "We're social creatures and music helps create communities, offering inclusive, meaningful social experiences."

"Music enables people to be contributors and not just recipients of care. It provides opportunities for people to reconnect with a sense of autonomy and agency, at times when they may feel as though they have little or no control because of the impact of dementia." (ClassicFM.com: 2019)

Over the years I have seen just how meaningful music can

be to many, and I too have felt the value and support from access music in my own time of need. As an activities coordinator I would often arrange musical sing-a-longs, in house entertainment, song quiz, musical Bingo, musical jam (we all practiced playing different instruments), Karaoke, "Care Home X Factor challenge" and the list goes on!

I know that music has been a great coping strategy for me, enabling me to switch off and take time out. One thing that was very person-centred that was available to residents in the home I was at, was personalised music play lists! These playlists would be created to enhance a "feel good" pick me up activity.

12. Art and Crafts – Free Art Friday

I absolutely love this and when I discovered this some years ago, I had to introduce this to the residents, who equality loved it as much as I did. "Free Art Friday is a global art movement, and here's how it works:
(as stated below in the article by Mic.com: 2019)

1. Create a piece of art. Drawing, painting, poetry, etc.
2. Write on an attached tag "*free art to take home and enjoy*" or something as lovely. Adding artist (or your care home name), email, or web address or social media tag is optional.
3. Place somewhere in public indoors or out. Easy or hard, it's up to you.
4. Some make a game out of it and leave clues on Twitter, Facebook, geocache, or make it a scavenger hunt.
5. It's NOT an exclusive group or movement, ANYBODY can join in. THIS MEANS YOU, and it's completely FREE!

So, get your arts, crafts, and sculpture activities in full flow and place them in your local community and follow the journey of this fabulous art movement. Check out the free art Friday community group on Facebook!

13. Rock On...And Explore Your Inner Rock Artist

We have provided many activities within care homes as activity coordinators and over the last few years we have delivered many community wellbeing projects. One element of our community project that is always in high demand is our wellbeing art activities. Paintings can come in all shapes and sizes, by utilising a diverse range of materials to create a super-duper masterpiece!

There are many ways to produce art from; traditional canvas, to hardboard or bits of driftwood to capture one's own creativity. But if you're stuck for inspiration, why not paint on a pebble?

The first thing to do is to choose your stone/pebble or rock! Those with a smooth surface work well. And if you don't fancy digging up your plants to look for a suitable candidate, you can always buy bags of pebbles from your local garden centre.

The best paints to use are a waterproof craft paint or acrylic. Ideally you should use two layers of vanish first, allow to dry, then proceed to paint your chosen design. Once your painting has dried, apply another coat or 2 of the vanish to seal, this will help to protect your painting. When it comes to planning and designing what you want to paint, use your imagination or alternatively check out "Pinterest" where you can discover a range of examples to provide you some inspirational ideas.

You will need a few things to begin with:
- Pebbles / Stones.

- Waterproof craft paint or acrylic paint.
- Paintbrushes.
- A glass of water.
- A colour mixing dish.
- Clear nail varnish / Glaze / Spray sealer.

(Please remember to seek professional medical advice before using any materials/chemicals that may cause an allergic reaction/ill health or in relation to any existing medically diagnosed conditions.)

Explore your inner creative rock artist, and when planning your ideas to paint, consider the shape and size of your rock or pebble as this can offer some inspiration too! Your rock might remind you of a tortoise, sparking your imagination. It's a great fun activity to do, one that you might want to consider doing when the grandchildren visit, as this can be a great family activity too! Once finished you may want to give your rock painting as a gift, use as paperweight or consider adding to the garden as a colourful garden ornament!

If you have painted a pebble, or feel inspired to give it a go, why not take a picture and share it with us on social media, using #ActivitiesGuru @MeaningfulEd on Twitter or @ Meaningful Education CIC on Instagram.

14. Aboriginal Art

Another popular activity within our wellbeing program is aboriginal art!

"Aboriginal art is the oldest form of artistic expression in the world. Art carvings found in the Northern Territory's Arnhem Land dates back at least 60,000 years. Using soil and rocks, artists are able to produce carvings, ground designs and paintings." (Culture Trip: 2019)

"It seems obvious, but aboriginal art is only considered Aboriginal if painted by someone who is of that origin." (Culture Trip: 2019)

We looked at a more conventional way of adapting this art form to our service users/ residents needs and abilities. We adopted the "Dot Painting" approach taken from the aboriginal art and culture. Our residents / service users were able to explore a different technique in relation to arts and learning a new way of painting. You can always use a template to guide you. We found using black card was very effective! You may feel confident to create your own freehand drawing, then use the dot technique to bring your creation to fusion.
Alternatively, you may want to use a stencil to create the outline of your chosen design. These look quite impressive once complete, an eye-catching display to bright up your home.

15. Residents Activity Planning Meeting

Yes, this is an activity in itself. This is a great opportunity to being residents together to participate in the planning of activities that they would like to be involved in (both within the home and out in the community). Keep the meeting informal, fun and engaging, with a focus on what activities residents would like to try, explore and continue to do. Ensure to cover a diverse range of activities to meet the needs, abilities and preference of all the residents when finalising your activities plan.

Here are some ideas to think about incorporating within your discussions:

- Social activities
- Events that will help raise funds for forthcoming activities.

- Discuss what the residents enjoy most
- New ideas on where's good to go on outings
- Celebrations and family time
- In-house activities
- Entertainment
- What is working well and what is not

Consider appointing a resident as the chairman/chairperson and appoint a carer to take minutes. Planning an agenda which you can hand out on the day will help to keep you on track and it is also good to be able to give residents a visual aid.

16. Read All About It

As an activity's coordinator working within dementia care, we would often discuss the news every morning. This was a very popular discussion. In fact, it grew to become a rather big daily activity! Every morning I would bring copies of the local and national newspapers in with me, and we would sit round in a big group and take it in turns to read a story or news headline and then discuss our thoughts and feeling on this, with a lovely supply of tea, coffee and of course biscuits.

There was a group of ladies (residents) who particularly enjoyed reading the dear Deirdre column, and it would often evoked lots of debates, and at times fits of laughter. I remember reading an article out loud to the female residents regarding a lady who had written in and she was talking about an embarrassing 1st date, and I remember as my eyes reading ahead, and I could see what was coming to my horror. The lady had written that on her first date when greeted by the gentleman and he said to her "nice to meet you and your camel toe!" To which a resident shouted out "What's a camel toe?" well I must admit I did go a little blush in the face and adults that we are I explained and the raw of laughter erupted within the lounge. In fact, a senior carer who was listening at the time almost spat her coffee out from the fits of laughter.

The different activities listed above are a great way to keep us active, socially, emotionally, physically and mentally. With a focus on reducing loneliness and isolation and to maintain independence. In our professional roles Clare and I do our best to keep on top of our own professional development, we read in our spare time, watch documentaries and also look after our own wellbeing by doing the things that we love and enjoy. We have discussed throughout the chapters how important it is to understand certain aspects of activities and why they are important, it is essential that the core needs are understood on a level where we recognise the need for growth and this what lead Clare and I to design and develop our signature course - MDA (Meaningful Daily Activities) training programme.

Our practical course provides you with the opportunity to learn how to facilitate a diverse range of activities in a safe learning environment, under the guidance and direction of our facilitator and will enable you to build your confidence to maintain a positive professional relationship with those within your care setting.

The theoretical learning explores how activities are planned and facilitated to meet the current care act regulations; this also includes how to implement evidence-based practice to meet current inspection standards.

CHAPTER 9
PHYSICAL EXERCISE

What is physical activity?

"Physical activity is defined as any bodily movement produced by skeletal muscles that requires energy expenditure" as stated by (World Health Organisation: 2019)

"The term 'physical activity' should not be mistaken with "exercise". Exercise is a subcategory of physical activity that is planned, structured, repetitive, and purposeful in the sense that the improvement or maintenance of one or more components of physical fitness is the objective. Physical activity includes exercise as well as other activities which involve bodily movement and are done as part of playing, working, active transportation, house chores and recreational activities."(World Health Organisation: 2019)

During my time as an activity co-coordinator and activities manager specializing in Mental Health and Dementia for the elderly, I had the privilege of attending the University of Birmingham. There I attended lectures and training and learnt about the effects of ageing and how to age well! During my time there I was also able to visit the Centre for Healthy Ageing Research and learnt about evidence-based research into practical applications to help minimise age-related musculoskeletal decline and disease. There are many benefits to keeping active, more so than ever as we age. Being active can help to:

- Improve mobility
- Prevent heart disease
- Improve posture
- Reduce risk of stroke
- Improve circulation
- Reduce stress
- Prevent depression
- Control weight
- Reduce arthritic pain & stiffness
- Reduce risk of falls
- Improve sleep
- Relieve constipation
- Improve mood
- Improve strength, power & balance

It can also be enjoyable, and often provides opportunities for social interaction which is fun and therefore, also beneficial for the person's well-being!

Putting it into practice

When planning physical activities, it is important to take a person-centred approach to meet the individual core needs, taking into consideration the individual's needs, abilities, choices and preferences. This does not have to be restricted to formal exercise programmes or activity groups. Every opportunity should be used to encourage physical activity and independence for example; engaging residents in making beds, helping to put things away, accessing outdoor spaces, gardening, helping with the daily upkeep of the home, after all it is THEIR HOME! Enabling a person to gain self-worth, and self-esteem and this will promote inclusivity in feeling connected to their environment and the people within it. Keeping active and regular exercise is also one of the best things that we can do as individuals to help reduce stress.

Over many years of directly supporting individuals, I have witnessed first-hand the struggles and difficulties people face when living with a diagnosis of dementia. These difficulties range from; Communication, Behavioural changes, memory loss; thinking and planning; place and person; learning; judgement; emotion; motivation, perception. These can all have an impact on a person's mobility and over all wellbeing.

As activity coordinators one thing that is often a struggle but, also a necessity is self-motivation. As coordinators we need a bucket full of motivation in order for us to efficiently apply ourselves to our job. We also need the ability to motivate others (residents and staff).

Motivation is the inner power that pushes you towards taking action and towards an achievement. When motivated you have the desire and 'can do' attitude to achieve your goals. But in times where we lack motivation, it is often due to the absence of desire and ambition. We lack the willingness to take the necessary action to achieve our desired goals. Motivation is powered by desire and ambition, and therefore, if they are absent, motivation is absent too.

When we are feeling full of motivation, it is because there is an initiative and direction, courage, energy, and the persistence to follow your goals. When you have a clear vision, precise knowledge of what you want to do, and a strong desire, and faith in our abilities, then Motivation will be present.

Ways in which to strengthen, encourage and maintain Motivation.

Set a goal, If you have a major goal, it would be a good idea if you split it into several minor goals, each small goal leading to your major goal.(like I explained in chapter 4 with setting goals for the RAF Veteran to work towards regaining an improved physical mobility) By dividing your goal into several, smaller goals, you will find it easier to motivate yourself, and your residents. As this will decrease any potential overwhelming feelings by the size of your overall end goal. This will also help you feel that the goal is more feasible, and easier to accomplish.

Going back to when I attended Birmingham University, it was during this time that I was able to learn and take part in the classes and demonstrations of "Move It or Lose It" and learn more about the importance of exercise as we age. Strength and balance exercises are vital for the 50's yet many are just not sure what they should be doing to maintain or improve their own well-being - Physically and Mentally, or what their options are? It is also important to be mindful that we are all aging and with the aging process it is important to reflect and evaluate on our own health, well-being, capabilities and mobility as we age, adapting and changing our own individual well-being strategies!

"Move it or lose it classes have been developed by experts to help you to improve your flexibility, agility, aerobic health, balance and strength for greater strength. All exercises can be done seated or standing depending on your ability." (moveitorlose.co.uk: 2019)

During our well-being week challenge I took Rigerta to visit a 'Move It or Lose' class. We were invited to take part in exercises at a community village hall. It was such a pleasure to meet the ladies attending the classes and they were highly motivating and inspirational, which made me realize that i really needed to improve my own fitness levels!

The exercise classes are very adaptable and can be chair-based exercises as I used to do with our residents! It is a really great workout with simple and easy to follow movements. I must admit I was really feeling the impact of the exercises in my arms and legs! Ouch! But in a good way of course!

As this was Rigerta's first time attending a 'Move it or Lose it' class, it was really good to see and hear about her experience too.

Rigerta said "I have heard so much about Move it or Lose it from my colleagues and I have seen the online tutorials of how the programme was facilitated. I thought it to be a fun way for people to exercise without the fast pace and impact on their bodies. However, this is where I was surprisingly wrong because as I did each of the exercises my body felt each and every single stretch and pull. I really feel there needs to be more Move it or Lose it classes everywhere as this is a great social experience and a great way to improve and maintain your well-being, physically and mentally. I really enjoyed myself and it's also about having fun!"

If you would like to discover more on this visit www.moveitorloseit.co.uk

Activities you may want to consider are:

1. Seated yoga

Yoga is a fantastic activity for improving strength and flexibility and helping to relax the mind. If your residents aren't particularly mobile, there are adapted yoga poses that can be done from the comfort of a chair. We'd recommend hiring a professional yoga teacher to help run these sessions.

2. Garden and floor games

Whether it's wet or dry outside, garden and floor games can be a great activity to do in a care home if you have the floor space. Skittles, boules, horseshoe and ring toss games are good as they can be played from a sitting position – perfect if your residents aren't that mobile.

3. Dance

The brilliance of dance as an exercise is its ability to bring together both movement and music into one activity. It has the power to stimulate reminiscence and is a great physical activity too. Don't worry too much about knowing the correct steps, simply ask your residents what their music preference is and get moving!

4. Tea Dance

I love a tea dance! A tea dance is a great social activity event that traditionally takes place in the afternoon, where people meet to dance and have tea and cake. Why not spice up your tea dance with a 'strictly come dancing' theme and have a judging panel too!

5. Folding laundry

Yes, that right, ask your residents if they would like to take part in domestic activities, from washing up, to folding laundry, hoovering and dusting. Many would have done these tasks within their daily living for many years and by providing these opportunities will enable a sense of purpose and self-worth that could help to boost their mood, self-confidence and self-worth.

6. Walking Group

Walking could make all the difference and It's a low impact activity, making it more accessible for many of your residents to get involved. You may want to consider creating your own residents walk and talk group! Most Health and leisure centres are providing many activities such as community walking groups and they have trained 'walk leaders' to help and support you and your residents along the way. If you are a wheelchair user, this is also of benefit as getting outdoors and being surrounded by nature is great for your wellbeing too. Before joining a walk, it is important to seek medical advice from a professional and to risk assess prior to the activity.

7. Dementia-friendly walks

There are many dementia friendly walking groups set up across the country that have been adapted to meet the needs of those living with a diagnosis of dementia. Dementia friendly walking groups will have volunteers who have been on training to become "dementia friends" or have attended dementia awareness courses, enabling them to fully understand how to support those individuals using the service. They also provide a higher number of walk leaders to support or service users.

If you would like to find your local group check out: www.walkingforhealth.org.uk

8. Men In sheds

Men in sheds provides "community spaces for men to connect, converse and create. The activities are often similar to those of garden sheds, but for groups of men to enjoy together. They help reduce loneliness and isolation, but most importantly, they're fun." (Menssheds.org.uk: 2019)

"A place to pursue practical interests at leisure, to practice skills and enjoy making and mending. The difference is that garden sheds and their activities are often solitary in nature while Men's Sheds are the opposite. They're about social connections and friendship building, sharing skills and knowledge, and of course a lot of laughter." (Menssheds.org.uk: 2019) This is a nation-wide scheme so do check out online to find your local group: www.mensshehttps://thewfa.co.uk/ds.org.uk

9. Walking football

"Walking football is different to regular Association Football in many ways and is aimed at the over 50's age group. Many tournaments are now catering exclusively for the over 60's age group.

It has very specific rules that outlaw all running and allows no contact between players. Over-head height restrictions and indirect free kicks ensure that the sport is played safely with full consideration to the participants' age.

Teams are either 5 or 6-a-side. As a result of these rules, games are played at a slower pace, often on state of the art 3G artificial grass pitches, thus reducing the threat of pain, discomfort and injury, with players briskly walking through matches. This allows people who have loved the sport all their lives to once again safely get back to playing and also introduces the sport to people who perhaps have never considered playing before." (The WFA 2019)

If you would like to discover your local walking football facility check out: www.thewfa.co.uk

10. Foot golf

"Footgolf is played on a golf course using a size 5 football. The object of the game is to get the ball into the hole using only your feet in the fewest number of shots possible.

Footgolf is a very 'addictive' sport - it combines the best of football and golf, two of the most popular sports in the world. The beauty of the game lies in you being able to strategically combine power and precision every time you play footgolf. And, of course, it is open to everyone." (UKfootgolf.com: 2019)

We have created many online links at the back of this book for you to explore these activities further. So, remember in order to keep active, maintain mobility and independence, you need to MOVE IT, or you will LOSE IT!

CHAPTER 10
DIGNITY, WHAT'S IT ALL ABOUT?

Dignity is a key human rights buzzword. It's something we all have, and which means we merit certain rights.

If we look briefly at the history and foundation of how dignity has evolved over the years starting with the "The Human Rights Act 1998 sets out the fundamental rights and freedoms that everyone in the UK is entitled to. It incorporates the rights set out in the European Convention on Human Rights (ECHR) into domestic British law. The Human Rights Act came into force in the UK in October 2000" (Equality and Human Rights Commission: 2019)

"The Act sets out your human rights in a series of 'Articles'. Below you will see each Article deals with a different right." (Equality and Human Rights Commission: 2019)

"These are all taken from the ECHR and are commonly known as 'the Convention Rights" (Equality and Human Rights Commission: 2019)

"Article:
2. Right to life
3. Freedom from torture and inhuman or degrading treatment
4. Freedom from Slavery and forced labour
5. Right to liberty and security

6. Right to a fair trial
7. No punishment without law
8. Respect for your private and family life, home and correspondence
9. Freedom of thought, belief and religion
10. Freedom of expression
11. Freedom of assembly and association
12. Right to marry and start a family
14. 14. Protection from discrimination in respect of these rights and freedoms"

"Protocol 1, Article 1: Right to peaceful enjoyment of your property
Protocol 1, Article 2: Right to education
Protocol 1, Article 3: Right to participate in free elections
Protocol 13, Article 1: Abolition of the death penalty"

"However, articles 1 and 13 of the ECHR do not feature in the Act. This is because, by creating the Human Rights Act, the UK has fulfilled these rights." (Equality and Human Rights Commission: 2019)

For example;

"Article 1 says that states must secure the rights of the Convention in their own jurisdiction. The Human Rights Act is the main way of doing this for the UK."

"Article 13 makes sure that if people's rights are violated, that they are able to access effective remedy. This means they can take their case to court to seek a judgment. The Human Rights Act is designed to make sure this happens." (Equality and Human Rights Commission: 2019)

Health and Social Care Act 2008 (Regulated Activities) Regulations 2014: Regulation 10

"The intention of this regulation is to make sure that

people using the service are treated with respect and dignity at all times while they are receiving care and treatment. To meet this regulation, providers must make sure that they provide care and treatment in a way that ensures people's dignity and treats them with respect at all times. This includes making sure that people have privacy when they need and want it, treating them as equals and providing any support they might need to be autonomous, independent and involved in their local community." (cqc.org.uk: 2019)

Protecting dignity from destruction: We use the term 'Inhumane' to describe acts that breach our basic human rights. An example would be acts such as torture which are prohibited because we want to protect and preserve the dignity and physical and mental integrity of individuals. In order to treat others humanely, means behaving towards them in a way that's consistent with preserving a person's dignity, and so dignity is something that we want to protect from destruction.

The right to health: Dignity is something that we want to help people achieve. In order for humanity to lead a dignified life it is paramount that there are basic human rights to adhere to. In this sense, dignity is something that we honour – by recognising that everyone has it.

"All human beings are born free and equal in dignity and rights." (Article 1 – United Nations: 2019)

"Everyone is entitled to all the rights and freedoms, without distinction of any kind, such as race, colour, sex, language, religion, political or other opinion, national or social origin, property, birth or other status." (Article 2 – United Nations: 2019)

Dignity is also often related to how we regard ourselves and can connect people from all kinds of cultures and beliefs, which has ultimately led to the universal recognition that we need to preserve and protect the dignity of others and within ourselves. So, as you can see from above there are many basic human rights and legislations that are fundamental to preserving the dignity of humanity.

I remember attending a local radio show where Rigerta and I were invited on to be guest speakers, to discuss the work that we do across the community. Anyone who knows me, knows I talk about dignity everywhere I go! I was so nervous; it was my first radio interview and we were to be there for the duration of an hour. I had all my notes prepared and I had an idea of what I wanted to say, until the first question was asked; "Why Dignity"? and before I knew it my mouth had engaged before brain and my response to this was "Why not Dignity?

How many times a day do you ask someone "Would you like a cup of tea or coffee, and how do you like it? Milk? Sugar?

You see if we talk about dignity (taking this simply everyday approach like asking who would like tea & coffee, it becomes a normal daily interaction) and if we understand what dignity means to our friends, family members, work colleagues and neighbours (you get the gist!) then we will become more aware of what dignity means to us individually, and how we can preserve a person's dignity in becoming more aware of our own actions and behaviours. When you have a deeper understanding of what dignity means to you as an individual and what it means to others it becomes a way of life, a part of your daily living, imbedded into your own culture! It becomes an inherent part of our behaviour, having dignity in your heart, mind and actions. Dignity is an important part of our daily lives and when neglected can be impactful on a person's well-being.

I am very committed and passionate about respecting people's dignity or as I like to refer to this as preserving a person's dignity. I know you can see from chapter one, that from very early on in my health and social care career, I was always very observant and challenged disrespectful or unkind behaviour, standing up for people's rights, more so when someone maybe unable to do so for themselves. But In order to truly understand the meaning of dignity, sometimes our own experiences often play a big part in this. At times when our dignity has been impacted upon negatively or disrespected, we may not truly understand, recognise or associate the emotions or feelings that relate to a lack of dignity. When I was in my teenage years, I lost the use of my legs for some time, and I was very unwell in hospital. In fact, I spent months in hospital and being unable to take myself to the toilet and needing help and support to wash and dress was very impactful on my own dignity. I cannot fault the hospital staff because I received the best care and support, they were amazing and so kind towards me, and I needed them.

But as I entered my adult life, sadly, I was to experience a difference in how I was treated, and an unpleasant one at that. You see, sometimes when we are unwell or seeking advice or support we can at times be and feel very vulnerable, and although we may feel like we want to speak up and challenge the way we have being treated, at that moment sometimes we are unable to for many reason. It often takes strength, courage and confidence to challenge someone when they have made you feel like they haven't treated you with dignity or respect. You see if we are unsure of what dignity means to us as an individual how can we expect others to preserve it? Also, we don't always recognise when our dignity has been impacted upon, nor do we associate it to our dignity. We will often recognise a feeling, an emotional connection, which leaves feelings of unsettlement, embarrassment, sadness, degraded, and often impacting on having certain rights taken from us, or a lack of choices.

I have spent many years exploring the meaning of dignity and analysed the individuality of this very important element across Humanity. From birth we begin our life dependant, and as we grow and develop, we gain our own independence, achieving a certain degree of autonomy, but such autonomy is never absolute. I have explored the meaning and value of dignity reaching out to all ages, diverse cultures, religions, genders, and Dignity has many different meanings to people from all walks of life. Dignity, as a term can be defined as an individualistic sentiment that makes us feel respected in our own right. Speaking from the term, 'in our own eyes', the dignity factor is bound to vary from one person to the next.

Dignity Matters, because it is a part of who we are, and it is part of our daily living. I would venture to say that dignity is also acting in a way that ensures one is viewed as acting in an appropriate manner to society. Ones actions should always come from a considered position that ensures appropriate behaviour in all circumstances.

I am not saying we are all expected to be perfect and get it right all of the time, however, I believe that human beings are capable of drifting in and out of human decency throughout their lives given particular circumstances.

In consideration of this, our actions matter, so it is important to be aware of our own actions. Preserving one's own dignity and being mindful of preserving the dignity in others. We all play a vital role within our communities; it is important to take the time to know your neighbours. There are many vulnerable and socially isolated individuals within our communities, no one should feel lonely and isolated when we live in an overpopulated world. Take the time to communicate, build positive relationships, get to know the people within your community, it is so important to feel valued and included within our society, conquer this and it will have long-lasting benefits in ones wellbeing and in the wellbeing of those that we connect with. Coming together as community would make our daily living a more meaningful and a pleasant place to be, which builds community cohesion.

What does Dignity mean to you? over the last 3 years this question has been asked to nearly every group of people we have either taught, spoken to, or facilitated a program for. When the question is asked its always the answer of 'I actually have never thought about it', in general how often if never do we question how we are greeted by other people, how they may pronounce our names, or some of the choices in which are made for us. Clare and I created the Bedfordshire Dignity Network back in 2016, I understood the concept of Dignity and I applied it by believing that the lack of independence alone was what would strip me of my Dignity. However, this was my belief at the time because I felt being independent was what was really important to me, don't get me wrong it still is, but I do not believe that I had a great understanding of what Dignity truly is. I had to make a decision in what it meant to me when we first started the BDN (Bedfordshire Dignity Network, when I say this, I mean I had to make a decision because I had never thought about it before. Throughout us campaigning for the last 3 years I have been in a position where I am asking other people what dignity truly means to them, what I have learnt from this is that it is very individualized and unique for every person as Clare has explained. When asked this question you will look at what is important to you, what are your expectations, and your morals and values in order to answer this question.

Each year we attend the Luton carnival in which we prepare all year long and we join our fellow colleagues to created what is known as the "health & wellbeing zone", this zone is made up of the different health and wellbeing organisations within Luton. We use this space to showcase what is currently available, coming together in one zone will give people more of an understanding of the services available. It is often difficult to find all of the services available as they are not all advertised in one place; therefore, the wellbeing zone offers fun activities and information for the whole family. It is also during this time that we promote the BDN campaign and this is where you truly start to understand how people interpret the word Dignity. Myself and Clare will proactively reach out and speak to attendees at the carnival with one question in mind - 'What does Dignity mean to you?' with our social media campaign we were inundated with responses, the one response which stuck with me and Clare was a man living with Dementia – and his response to us was,

'Just because I have Dementia doesn't mean I can't be a part of my community, I want to be treated with Respect & Dignity and included like anyone else, I may have an illness but I'm still me and I'm still part of this community'.

We are in the same community together and for that reason alone I feel it is very important to treat each other with respect and dignity all round. We are different and we come from different backgrounds, different religions, and also a different way of upbringing. However, that does not make us better than anybody else and that does not give us any right to behave in a way that implies we are better than anybody else. As a society we are quick to make judgement on ways of living in which do not match our own, the way in which other people live does not necessarily mean it is wrong or out of the ordinary, we are all living on the factors of our own upbringing. Whilst you may think the way you are living life is perfect, another person may disagree as they have different factors in which make them who they are, this is where dignity and respect is very important to understand.

During our time writing this book, about topics that have

so much power, meaning, and value. Whilst discussing Dignity (as we do daily) I explained to Clare that within Albanian/Montenegrin culture we respect our elders more than anything. We are not allowed to talk back or question what they are saying, we can have debates and discussions but it is seen as a sign of disrespect if you do not address them as your elder, when saying this I also mean in how we address them by name. My mothers and fathers' brothers and sister (siblings), I would be expected to address them as aunt and uncle, if it is my uncles' wife I would have to say 'dada' before their name as a sign of respect. My mother is the youngest in her family and she will be called 'teta' before her name, as would I around some of my nieces and nephews. Clare coming from a British culture said to me that till this day she still call's her elder's –"aunts and uncles" as a sign of respect, when people ask about our backgrounds this is one aspect that people need to understand wholesomely as identified when having these conversation we recognized a commonality in that we share a lot of the same morals and values. It is amazing to see how two women from two different cultures have come together based on the same principles, morals and values, with the same aim of changing people's lives for the better.

When discussing dignity, I (Rigerta) can say that I have come to a decision on what it truly means to me. I love my background and where I am from as an individual, it is who I am and what has influenced many and if not all of my decisions in my life so far. My dignity for me is my personal space when I go to the core of it, what I regard as personal space is me, myself and I and who I allow within that space, which is entirely my choice. Within cultures it is normal to hug and kiss one another on the cheek when greeting each other and saying goodbye, in some cultures even if you are not family members but within Albanian/Montenegrin culture and religion it is not the norm. I have over the years found this difficult when it has come to meeting new people as it makes me feel a little uncomfortable, I have as of now decided to let people know that I do not do that within my culture and religion and I would wish for them to respect that. Knowledge and understanding is where as a community we can fully start to respect each other, as I have mentioned it does not mean that it is wrong but everyone is different and we all have factors in which answers the question 'what does dignity mean to you'. It is individual and it is our choice in what that means to each and every single one of us.

"A life of dignity means you are as valuable and important, worthy and wanted, as any other human being. It means, fundamentally, that you matter. And when you believe you matter, then you know that your voice matters, your relationships matter, and your actions matter." (global dignity: 2019)

As carers and activity coordinators we are in a particular role of trust, and we need to always make sure that we act in the best interest of those within our care, and at times that means having the confidence to act and stand up and champion dignity within your care setting. As an activity's coordinator or carer, whatever your role, it is about having a positive impact, working with others to transform your care setting or within your community into one where understanding, compassion and kindness triumph. You can be a change maker, or what we call a **Dignity Champion!**

ABOUT THE AUTHORS

Clare Copleston has a demonstrated history of working within the Health & Social Care industry with over 16 years' experience, specialising in activity provisions, dementia care and mental health services in both public and private health care.

Clare completed her degree at the University of Bedfordshire and is now a teacher of Mental Health Studies, including care act standards, and a visiting lecturer at the university for undergraduates. Clare is a director at Meaningful Education Ltd. CIC and is the founder of the Bedfordshire Dignity Network.

Clare believes that every human being has the right to lead a dignified life, and that we all have a common responsibility and opportunity to strengthen the dignity of others. Dignity should be the foundation for human interaction, and she is fully dedicated to improving and raising awareness of the importance of our actions and how it may impact others. Clare's passion to write this book was to shine the light on activity coordinators and carers – the unsung heroes in health and social care.

A message from Clare…

"I truly understand first-hand how hard it is to facilitate these roles and responsibilities and I want you to know that you are appreciated, you are amazing and we need more activity coordinators who are dedicated, compassionate, kind and caring. More so now than ever with the increasing demand and need for health and social care services across Great Britain."

Clare, a dedicated dignity champion and a mental health activist, who is compassionate and committed to helping and supporting others to enable a meaningful daily living through activity provisions, shines vibrantly throughout this book.

Rigerta Ahmetaj achieved her degree in Marketing with Advertising at Hertfordshire University and has extensive experience as an interpreter, teacher, and community volunteer within Public Health, Local Authority and Social Service sectors specialising in mental health, education, clinical services and immigration. Rigerta is a Co-Director at Meaningful Education Ltd. CIC.

Rigerta is committed to creating positive change within communities, which is demonstrated by the extensive work and projects that she delivers across Bedfordshire and beyond. Her passion is to raise awareness and to educate children and young people to understand mental health and break down stigma within society.

A message from Rigerta...

"Three children in every classroom have a diagnosed mental illness, according to the charity Young Minds. We need to equip our children and young people with the tools, resources and understanding of how they can look after their mental health and well-being. Activities are a fundamental part of our daily living and we need to accept that's its ok not to be ok and to reach out and ask for help and support when needed."

Rigerta aims to empower local communities to create a movement of positive well-being through activities and support, changing people's lives for the better, and building community cohesion in order to decrease social isolation.

Do follow them on their Facebook page for more info **@activitygurus**.

TESTIMONIALS

"Clare is an amazing tutor and her delivery techniques are fantastic."

L.C – Cares Academy student

"I cannot imagine a better course. It is so helpful. Clare is a wonderful lady and I will miss this course and, the people. It has been an amazing experience."

M.K – Carers Academy student

"This course has motivated me to learn more and to be interested in more things. I have gained a deeper self-awareness and have learnt that its ok not to be ok, and to recognise how I am feeling. Clare and Rigerta have given me a tremendous amount of support and have helped me a lot. I am proud to have attended the whole course."

L.M – Carers Academy student

"What has been great is the experience and knowledge that Clare shares, connecting real life experiences and situations to enable a better understanding. Clare really understands the struggles people go through, and she is caring, understanding and empathetic. She treats people with dignity and respect. I would attend any future course by Meaningful Education Ltd."

CIC.
S.K – Understanding Dementia course – Student feedback

"Clare, thank you for such a wonderful speech. I connected with each and every word you said. I truly felt a connection and it empowered me immensely. It's all about the mindset!"

Women Like Me conference

"Thank you so much for giving such a heartfelt and empowering speech. It propelled me to ask myself so many questions. Thank you for sharing yourself, you definitely challenged me in more ways than you could imagine! You are an inspirational and empowering woman."

Women Like Me conference

"Thank you for providing me with opportunities and for supporting me. Meaningful Education has helped me to grow my confidence and life skills. I feel very happy and privileged to be part of a great team."

Josh - Volunteer

"The courses run by Meaningful Education are very well delivered and extremely informative."

N Shadbolt

"I had a lot of fun discovering different aspects of both directors (Clare and Rigerta). For example, when they are in the office, they like to create a nice and relaxed environment but when they are teaching, they like to be very serious and professional about their work."

Karolina – Work experience

"The training today gave me a boost, with fantastic ideas and new ways to better my documentation"

Tarmara – Meaningful Daily Activities training

"Resources provided by Meaningful Education were amazing. It's fantastic knowing that there is great encouragement that I can take away from this training."

Amanda – Meaningful Daily Activities training

"Clare and Rigerta are very friendly. The training provided a wonderful and positive learning environment, and I am so happy and grateful. I think every part of the course was essential for me."

Muhfuza – Meaningful Daily Activities training

REFERENCES

Chapter 2
https://www.criminalrecordsservices.com/crb-dbs-explained/

Chapter 3
https://www.dignityincare.org.uk/Dignity-Champions/

Chapter 4
https://www.gov.uk/government/organisations/care-quality-commission
https://www.tonyrobbins.com/mind-meaning/do-you-need-to-feel-significant/
https://www.cqc.org.uk/

Chapter 5
https://www.hse.gov.uk/stress/mental-health.htm
https://www.who.int/mental_health/in_the_workplace/en/
https://www.sciencedaily.com/releases/2018/08/180808193656.htm
https://www.nhs.uk/conditions/stress-anxiety-depression/improve-mental-wellbeing/
https://hotpodyoga.com/our-classes/
https://www.independent.co.uk/life-style/health-and-families/loneliness-lethal-condition-therapy-psychology-cox-commission-ons-health-a8311781.html
https://www.hse.gov.uk/stress/mental-health.htm

Chapter 6
https://www.christianity.com/church/church-life/what-is-

ash-wednesday-why-do-christians-celebrate-it.html
https://www.learnreligions.com/diwali-festival-of-lights-1770151

Chapter 8
https://www.nhs.uk/conditions/stress-anxiety-depression/ways-relieve-stress/
https://www.mentalhealth.org.uk/publications/how-look-after-your-mental-health-using-mindfulness
https://www.psychologytoday.com/gb/blog/the-psychology-dress/201111/visualize-it
https://www.alzproducts.co.uk/a-sense-of-calm-2-dvd-soc-0002dvd
https://www.asenseofcalm.com/index.html
https://www.homecare.co.uk/news/article.cfm/id/1572656/ReminiScent-cards-evoke-memories-and-stimulate-conversation-for-those-living-with-dementia
https://www.scie.org.uk/dementia/living-with-dementia/keeping-active/reminiscence.asp
https://supercarers.com/blog/keep-your-pets-close-how-animals-help-dementia/
https://www.classicfm.com/discover-music/music-for-people-living-with-dementia-isnt-nicety/
https://www.mic.com/articles/30569/free-art-friday-a-global-art-movement-everyone-can-appreciate
https://theculturetrip.com/pacific/australia/articles/10-things-you-should-know-about-aboriginal-art/

Chapter 9
https://www.who.int/dietphysicalactivity/pa/en/
https://thewfa.co.uk/
www.thewfa.co.uk
https://www.moveitorloseit.co.uk/
http://www.ukfootgolf.com/about/4587215539

Chapter 10
https://www.equalityhumanrights.com/en/human-

rights/human-rights-act

CQC; 2019

https://www.cqc.org.uk/guidance-providers/regulations-enforcement/regulation-10-dignity-respect
https://www.equalityhumanrights.com/en/human-rights/human-rights-act

Article 1 & 2 – United nations

https://www.un.org/en/universal-declaration-human-rights/

Global Dignity: 2019

https://globaldignity.org/

ECHR

https://www.echr.coe.int/Pages/home.aspx?p=home

Other:

https://www.abbeyfield.com/2019/04/the-importance-of-sensory-activities-for-those-living-with-dementia/
https://www.psychologytoday.com/gb/basics/creativity
https://extension.psu.edu/programs/betterkidcare/early-care/tip-pages/all/childrens-art
https://www.aarp.org/content/dam/aarp/health/brain_heal
th/2017/07/gcbh-cognitively-stimulating-activities-report-english-aarp.doi.10.26419%252Fpia.00001.001.pdf
https://www.rhinouk.com/blog/the-benefits-of-multi-sensory-environments/
https://www.nestle.co.uk/en-gb/aboutus/history/reminiscence-pack
https://www.mic.com/articles/30569/free-art-friday-a-global-art-movement-everyone-can-appreciate
https://www.bbc.co.uk/bitesize/topics/ztkxpv4/articles/zvf
nkmn
https://ec.europa.eu/health/non_communicable_diseases/m
ental_health/eu_compass_en
https://inews.co.uk/news/i-lost-job-wife-home-depression-

now-i-give-mental-health-training-businesses/
https://www.equalityhumanrights.com/en/human-rights/human-rights-act
https://www.cqc.org.uk/guidance-providers/regulations-enforcement/regulation-10-dignity-respect
https://www.cqc.org.uk/sites/default/files/20150510_hsca_2008_regulated_activities_regs_2104_current.pdf

Technology Activities Resources
Reminiscence and family interaction

http://www.mybrainbook.com/login
http://memoryboxnetwork.org/
http://ireminisce.co.uk/reminiscence-therapy-activities
http://ireminisce.co.uk/
http://www.memory-bank.org/
http://www.remindmecare.com/pricing-for-care-homes

Activity links
https://www.walkingforhealth.org.uk/walkfinder
https://menssheds.org.uk/
https://thewfa.co.uk/
http://www.ukfootgolf.com/about/4587215539

Further links and resources
For more information about ReminiScent and the Smell & Connect cards, visit: http://smellandconnect.co.uk/.

https://www.awarenessdays.com/

Printed in Great Britain
by Amazon